Collecting
ANTIQUE BIRD
DECOYS
AND
DUCK CALLS

An Identification and Value Guide
by
Carl F. Luckey

ISBN 0-89689-078-3

BOOKS AMERICANA

DEDICATION

For J.W.B.
A friend is one who knows you as you are, understands where you've been, accepts who you've become—and still, gently invites you to grow.

ACKNOWLEDGEMENTS FOR THE DECOY SECTION

First Edition

Grateful acknowledgement is given to Dick McIntyre of Fripp Island, South Carolina for his seemingly tireless effort in educating me in the ways of old decoys and allowing invasion of his home more than once, to photograph his collection. Thanks also to collectors Don Drennon of Birmingham, Alabama and Neal and Patty Clement for their generosity and patience while photographing their decoys.

Second Edition

Special thanks are due Scott Higgins, Armdale, Nova Scotia, Canada; Bonnie Pover of the Noyes Museum, Oceanville, NJ; Lou Razek of the Highwood Bookshop, Traverse City, MI; Robert Shaw of the Shelburne Museum, Shelburne, VT; Hal Sorenson, Burlington, Iowa; and Charles Wechsler, editor, *Sporting Classics* magazine, Camden, SC.

ACKNOWLEDGEMENTS FOR THE DUCK CALL SECTION

A very large measure of hearty and heartfelt thanks goes to Howard Harlan of Nashville, Tennessee for his generous gift of time educating me in the world of duck call collecting and allowing me to photograph a portion of his collection.

Special thanks also to Tom Barré of Pocahontas, Arkansas for letting me interfere with business to photograph his duck calls during and between sales and trades at the Reelfoot Lake Wildlife Festival, 1991.

Thanks are due also to Russell Caldwell, Union City Tennessee, for his help and encouragement, and to the late J.L. Melancon of Robeline, LA; W.F. "Tom" Dennison, Newbern, TN; and Wendell R. Carlson of Cedar Rapids, IA for their very generous contributions.

CONTENTS

COLLECTING DECOYS

Introduction 1
A Short History of the American Bird Decoy 3
Some Thoughts on Decoys 5
The Decoy Collector 6
Dictionary of Terminology 7
Collecting Decoys 15
Identification of Antique Decoys 15
Brands 16
Decorative and Reproduction Decoys 23
Misrepresentations, Forgeries and Fakes 26
Restoration and Repairs 27
Value Determination 27
Some Major Factors That Determine The Value of Old Decoys 28
Care of Your Collection 30
Decoy Dealers and Collectors 32
Decoy Auctions 33
Publications for Decoy Collectors 34
Recommended Books for Collectors 35
Maps of Selected Areas 40
The Schools of Carvers 46
    Nova Scotia 47
    Maine 49
    Massachusetts 51
    Connecticut (Stratford) 56
    New York State 60
    Long Island 64
    Barnegat (New Jersey) 67
    Delaware River 73
    Susquehanna Flats 78
    Maryland Eastern Shore 89
    Crisfield (Maryland) 91
    Virginia Eastern Shore 96
    Cobb Island 106
    North Carolina 112
    South Carolina 118
    Louisiana 123
    Illinois River 126
    Michigan 131
    St. Clair Flats 137
    Wisconsin 142
    Pacific Coast 145

Factory Decoys 148
    J.N. Dodge 149
    Evans Duck Decoy Company 151
    Herters, Inc 154
    Mason's Decoy Factory 156
    William E. Pratt Manufacturing Company 165
    H.A. Stevens 167
    Victor Animal Trap Company 170
    Wildfowler Decoys, Inc 172

COLLECTING DUCK CALLS

Introduction 183
Identification and Evaluation of Calls 185
Construction and Nomenclature of Calls 186
Books and Other Publications about Calls 189
A History of Duck and Game Calls 191
Index 228

INTRODUCTION

There are many ways to approach the idea of collecting decoys. There are dozens and dozens of known carvers and factories. There are, of course, also dozens of species of birds represented, as well as many different hunting areas and major flyways. With this in mind the collector may choose to specialize in one of the areas. For instance, you might wish to concentrate on decoys that are indigenous to the area you live in, a particular species of bird, factory made decoys, etc. Another very satisfying way of collecting is to obtain any decoy within your means that simply pleases you.

There are three major groups of decoys. They are defined as to maker.

1. **Commercially produced** are those decoys carved and painted by hand for sale purposes.

2. **Non-commercially produced** decoys are those produced by a hunter for his own or friends' use and not sold as a rule.

3. **Factory produced** decoys are those made in a commerical facility, usually turned out in great numbers by machine lathes.

In this presentation the first two categories will be lumped together as hand-carved decoys, and factory-made decoys will be treated separately from them. Each section will present detailed discussions of these categories.

Most decoy collectors refer to certain geographic areas where decoys were carved and hunted over as "Schools" of decoy makers. There are probably thirty or more identifiable schools of carvers in the various flyways, but for the purpose of simplification this book will present only about twenty of the major areas or schools wherein the carvers lived and worked. The information and photographs will attempt to give you some basic tools that should enable you to look at a particular decoy and at least identify what part of the country it is from. The discussion and the photographs within each school are chosen to give you construction techniques and painting styles that are typical of that school. Please keep in mind that this book in no way attempts to cover all makers, but to present one or more makers from each region or school whose work exhibits the more typical characteristics of that school.

The general information presented in the first pages of the book will provide you with valuable identification data and prepare you for the more technical data included in the discussion of each major school of carvers.

Factory made decoys will be covered in much the same way.

The value information associated with the listing will be presented in ranges and, in many cases, widely varying ranges. The value ranges are given merely as a guide and most of them have been derived from auction catalogs and dealers sales lists. Given the present state of our economy and its result on the entire collectibles market and wildly ranging auction results, these values must be treated only as a starting point in the arrival at the value of a particular decoy.

When using the value ranges in this book it is incumbent upon the collector to bear in mind several factors, not the least of which is aptly put by a noted collector of old fishing lures, Clyde Harbin, "The Bass Man": "Nothin' ain't worth nothin', 'til somebody wants it." It really doesn't matter what the value placed on it here, if you don't want it the value is academic; if you do, however, you might be willing to pay more than the high end of the value range listed. There are many other factors influencing values. If, for instance, there is a particularly rare and hard-to-find decoy known to exist only in four or five collections and suddenly, however unlikely, a group of twenty to twenty-five is found in an old barn loft and offered for sale at auction the resulting prices realized might be considerably less than the heretofore accepted value.

Marks on the decoy can also affect value and condition can have a heavy influence. The values presented with the listings here are for decoys in good to excellent condition.

There is a tendency for collectors to take a book such as this one and use it as the final authority. That is foolhardy. The collector must use this book in conjunction with his own experience, the word of a trusted dealer, and all the other sources of value information he can get his hands on; dealer lists, periodical articles, sales ads, auction lists, etc. Remember the values listed here are first of all, just one man's opinion and secondly, they are for a given period of time. Delays inherent in publication make the values a valid opinion for a period of time just prior to publication and release of the book.

A SHORT HISTORY OF THE BIRD DECOY IN NORTH AMERICA

The origin of the decoy as we know it today lies in early American history, but not with the early settlers as might be reasonably assumed. Rather it pre-dates the American pioneer by at least one thousand, perhaps two thousand years. In 1924 at an archeological site in Nevada, the Lovelock Cave excavations, yielded a group of eleven decoys beautifully preserved in protective containers. Among this group of decoys were some stuffed skins, but there were eleven totally artificial decoys fashioned of twisted and bundled tule rushes or bullrushes (reeds) and feathers in a startlingly realistic form that is unmistakably that of a Canvasback duck. The careful manner of their storage preserved them for us to enjoy an estimated one to two thousand years later. More importantly, the extreme care the early Indians took in the preservation of their duck decoys suggests the critical importance to them of duck hunting, and the obtaining of the meat of wildfowl must have been an important factor in their survival.

When the first settlers came to North America their survival was just as dependent upon hunting wild game for food as were the Indians. It didn't take them long to notice the various methods the Indians used to lure wildfowl within bow and arrow range. They used a little of everything, from piles of rocks to clumps of mud and dead birds to make likenesses of their prey. Quick to seize upon the idea, those early settlers just as quickly improved it. They began to fashion likenesses of their prey out of different materials, ultimately finding that wood was an ideal raw material. Thus the carving of wildfowl decoys was born.

It isn't likely that those early Americans carved a bird likeness and then said, "Ah ha, a decoy." The lures were called many things but the word "decoy" was not yet in their vocabulary. Just when the word did come into common use is not precisely known buts its etymology or origin is known. Its roots are European, in particular Dutch. Decoy is derived from the Dutch word used to describe a cage-like affair into which the birds were driven by hunters in boats. Later domesticated ducks were placed inside to lure unsuspecting wildfowl into it. The name given to this cage was **ende-kooi**. This method was used before the advent of guns in wildfowl hunting.

Among the first writings of North American hunting to mention decoys was a letter from an official of the government of the then French colony of Newfoundland dated 1687. In describing a hunting expedition, he detailed a blind he called a "Hutt" and went on to say: "For a decoy they have the skins of geese, Bustards, and ducks, dry'd and stuff'd with Hay. The two feet being made fast with two Nails to a small piece of a light plank, which floats around the Hutt." Historical records indicate wooden decoys were in general use as early as the 1770's, but it seems likely they would have been widely used before then.

Up to the middle of the 1800's there was not sufficient commercial demand for decoys to enable the carvers to make a living at selling them, so most decoys were made for themselves and friends. The middle of the nineteenth century saw the birth of the "market gunners." These men were in the business of providing markets with the hundreds of thousands of birds necessary to feed the increasing North American population. These hunters, using huge guns and much of the time deploying rigs of hundreds of decoys, killed hundreds of birds of any sort in one outing. There were no game laws at the time and the seemingly inexhaustible supply of wildfowl provided them with a living and the overcrowded and, for the most part, poor emigrant poplulation of the larger eastern seaboard cities with relatively cheap meat. The market hunters and other hunters killed anything that flew, from Red Breasted Robins and Passenger Pigeons to the majestic Heron and Whistling Swan. Their activities are usually associated with the Chesapeake Bay area, but this slaughter was taking place in all the major flyways. The sad result of this indiscriminate destruction of wildfowl is that the coup de grace was administered to many bird species, rendering them extinct. Some others are on the endangered list as a result. A few examples are:

the Passenger Pigeon, Labrador Duck and the Heath Hen. The killing of wildfowl for sale was outlawed by the United States Congress with their passing of the Migratory Bird Treaty Act in 1918.

During that period of time many carvers were to begin making a living with their decoys and the first factory-made decoys came into existence. The huge numbers of decoys required to supply the market hunters (who often utilized 500-600 decoys at a time) and the rising numbers of single hunters for sport or sustenance made commercial decoy carving possible.

Following the passage of the 1918 act came the demise of the factory decoys of the day. The large numbers of decoys needed declined because of the act and many of the smaller commercial carvers had ceased to ply their trade by the 1920's. There were a few of these small, one or two-man or family operations that continued to carve birds, and with the great increase in the popularity of sport hunting the commercial carvers soon found the demand for their production rising. Some of these craftsman continued to work right on up into the 1950's. Today their tradition is carried on by a few truly great contemporary carvers. The latter produce incredibly intricate, life-like birds. The serious contemporary carvers' products have to meet strenuous requirements, making the decoy such that it **could** be hunted over. The prices these carvings command make it unlikely that they will float anywhere but in a competition water tank. What these contemporary carvings represent is that decoy carving is one of the few early American folk arts that has survived into our modern fast-paced times and still being pursued.

SOME THOUGHTS ON DECOYS

The first synthetic material used to construct decoys was rubber and this was as far back in the history of decoy making as 1867. It obviously didn't have much effect on the carvers of the day, but it serves as a harbinger of what was to come. In man's indefatigable search for an easier way, less talented individuals and/or those more business-minded, began to use other synthetics. The canvas, pressed or composite wood or other synthetic, paper mache, and plastics most of which is used in the manufacture of gunning decoys have pressed the old hand-carved ones out of service for the most part, and into antique shops, collectors' hands and dark cellars, attics, garages and boat houses, the latter being the last deposits of many a fine old gunning block. In the early days of their discard many, sadly, went the way of the stove for firewood.

A good many of those old treasures probably still reside where they were last deposited. While the likelihood of discovering one of those caches or finding a bargain at an estate sale or yard sale is diminished, the possibility still exists; especially so in areas removed from where hunting wild fowl and decoy making was heavy. Not long ago a man bought an old wood-worker's chest and in it found some fine old decoys that brought substantial money at auction. Around the same time a hunting club, needing to raise money, sold a rig of several dozen disused decoys for one thousand dollars. Several very valuable decoys that brought a great deal of money were found among those in the rig. Although the great pleasure derived from such finds can't be discounted, the true collector gains most of his satisfaction from the look and feel of his blocks, the beauty and appeal, and the handling of a well crafted decoy. The true collector's appreciation is enhanced by his knowledge that the decoys in his collection were made by the knowledgeable hands of an artist and craftsman who was also a skilled hunter who understood the importance of the concept of distinguishing marks, colors and shapes, the rendering of a decoy with simplicity of design rather than as an exact copy. Anything more than that in a decoy is strictly for the maker's self-satisfaction or for the hunter's eyes, not for the prey. Harry Walsh, in Chapter II of ***The Outlaw Gunner**, "Gunning with Decoys," put it succinctly: "Most decoys are painted more for the hunter than for the ducks." There will be arguments about this as long as there are hunters using decoys, but the fact that most manufacturers of today produce relatively simple decoys may be the statement of a silent concensus.

In 1918, the passage of the Migratory Bird Treaty act caused the almost immediate demise of the factories that made decoys and most of the hand makers even quit. The treaty was to stop the wholesale destruction wrought by the market gunners as we have discussed, but it seemed to take the spirit out of the sport hunters. Up until then decoys were rarely considered anything but tools to help hunt wildfowl. The 1920's and 1930's saw a resumed and increased popularity of sport hunting. Around that time more and more makers and hunters were beginning to appreciate them for their beauty. As a result a few talented makers began carving and painting a few decoys with great detail faithful to the real thing. These represent the birth of contemporary carving of decorative decoys. The use of the word "decorative" to describe these fine works of art is not meant to imply any disdain for them, it is merely to distinguish them from the true gunning decoy. While they are required to meet many stringent criteria in competition judging that would make them very good gunning decoys, they are not meant to be hunted over. It is that same period of time when more than just hunters were beginning to recognize beauty as well as utilitarian value in decoys. Curators of museums began obtaining them and placing them in their "Primitive" collection. One has to wonder why the "primitive" appellation when the sheer beauty of so many of them was so obviously far from primitive. In any case they have finally been given their proper recognition. Indeed there are now even entire wings of museums and buildings, and multi-million dollar auctions now given over to decoy collections.

*The Outlaw Gunner. Copyright 1971, Tidewater Publishers, Cambridge, Maryland.

THE DECOY COLLECTOR (Hoardbirdens enmassus)

I don't know whether Mike Beno coined the phrase or not, but his reference to *"Hoardbirdens enmassus," a tongue-in-cheek pseudo-scientific name for the decoy collector is both amusing and appropriate.

The genus and species Hoardbirdens enmassus can be found in all habitats, in all sorts of decorated forms and shapes, and tends to erratic migration. Its call is characterized by various chuckles, screams and exclamations in variations of words sounding like "bird," "block," "toller," "stool," "decoy," or "dee-coy." What all these critters have in common is a voracious appetite and their nests are usually overflowing with their prey, the decoy.

The collecting of decoys is growing in great leaps and bounds today but there have been serious collectors around since Joel Barber first wrote about them from a collecting point of view in his 1934 book, **Wild Fowl Decoys**. Barber is acknowledged by collectors as the granddaddy of decoy collecting. After Barber's book the hobby grew fairly slowly with a few new names popping up from time to time over the years since. It seems that his writings unearthed a larger group of afficionados than he himself realized existed. Names like Mackey, Starr, Sorenson and many others have become legendary among collectors. These were among the first to have written extensively about decoys and collecting. Since then many more have come along with excellent scholarly works for collectors. These will be mentioned later as recommended references.

That these writers have taken such pains to document North American decoys and their makers is evidence enough of decoys as a legitimate collectible. There is further overwhelming evidence that they are not only eminently collectible but that they also enjoy a distinguished status as a truly original American folk art. That status is incontestable when you look at the decoy's inclusion in many fine museum collections and the number of auctions, shows and sales annually devoted exclusively to decoys.

Decoys represent a unique form in American folk art history in that they have a property not common in that genre; they were never intended to be pretty. On the contrary, they were first and foremost made to serve a purely utilitarian function-to lure wildfowl within killing distance of the hunter. If the working decoy turned out to be beautifully carved and painted, it probably was simply for the self-satisfaction of the maker's own artist tendencies. Some contend that the beautiful ones may have been decorated for the individual user rather than the wildfowl hunted. This may be true to some extent now, but because most of the early makers produced them more for their own or friends use than for commerical advantage, they were probably shaped and painted on the theory that the more they appeared like the real thing, the more effective they would be. Some makers were more adept at this than others.

The earliest collectors were generally sportsmen who appreciated the aesthetics of decoys as well as the fond memories of hunting over them. These feelings ring out in their writings. This is not always so. Indeed, Joel Barber never even hunted wildfowl in his life. His appreciation was solely for the art form and of their importance as American folk art.

One can readily see that there were huge numbers of decoys produced during the heyday of market hunting by both carvers and factories, but they are fast being snapped up by collectors. One thing that should be pointed out is that many of them went the way of firewood or even landfill after the passage of the 1918 Act and there may not be as many around as might be assumed at first thought.

*In an article in *Ducks Unlimited* magazine, Sept./Oct. 1982, **A Poet, A Painter, A Whittler of Wood**, by Mike Beno.

DICTIONARY OF TERMINOLOGY

The following pages introduce you to terminology you will encounter in the remainder of this book and in dealing with other collectors and sellers. Careful study and constant reference to it will give you a working knowledge of the terminology, hence making it easier to read sales and auction lists and to describe your pieces to other collectors.

Some terminology listed here is elementary and some even obvious, especially to hunters. They are here because many collectors or would-be collectors are not hunters and may not be familiar with the terms.

ANCHOR LINE TIE—These are as varied as the men who carved decoys. There were screw-eyes, leather loops, or simply nails. The makers used whatever was available but some used the same type most of the time, giving the collector another clue as to the origin of a decoy. It should be pointed out here over the years of use a hunter may have altered or changed the line tie to suit himself.

BALLAST—Some decoy makers used ballast to make the decoy more stable in the water. In some cases the ballast is incorporated into a keel, but most are simply weights attached to the bottom in some manner. A few makers had a distinctive method for attaching them, helping in identifying the decoy. The weights vary from anything heavy lying around, such as pieces of horseshoes or any chunk of metal, to a well made lead or iron casting. Some were attached before painting, some after, and some consisted of molten lead poured into a cavity hollowed out for the purpose by the maker. There was one school in the Mississippi Flyway in which are found decoys with a swing keel with the ballast at the end, much like some small trailerable sailboats use today. Don't forget that many hunters applied their own ballast or weights, or they may have been removed, so it is not always a reliable indicator of maker or school.

BANJO TAIL—A style of carving usually associated with the Virginia Eastern Shore school of carvers and in particular with Ira Hudson. Appears somewhat like the fret of a banjo.

PLATE 1. An Ira Hudson Hooded Merganzer drake showing the Banjo Tail.

BATTERY [Boat]—See SINK BOX

BATTERY GUN—See PUNT GUN

BLOCK—A term sometimes used to mean decoy. Apparently this usage is derived from the block of wood a carver begins with in creating a decoy.

BOTTOM BOARD—Many decoys are found with a hollowed-out body and a flat board fitted to the bottom to seal it off and provide a base. The use and sometimes the thickness of a board can be a clue to maker or school in some cases.

BRANDS—A word used to describe a broad spectrum of marks to be found on decoys. They can range from simple carved initials all the way to complicated company logos. For a detailed description of brands, see pages 16 through 22.

CHECKING—This is the cracking of wood due to the natural oils and moisture drying or evaporating over the years.

COMB FEATHER PAINTING—This is a method of painting a decoy wherein the maker will paint the final coat and set the decoy aside to partially dry. When the paint reaches the proper consistency the maker then uses a comb or comb-like instrument to scratch feather patterns into the paint. This gives a very realistic texture to the finished product.

CONFIDENCE DECOY—William Mackey in his **American Bird Decoys** contends that "...the only true 'confidence' decoy is a gull decoy." He goes on to give swan decoys some credit to the title. The confidence decoy is truly a decoy of any species of bird that can instill confidence in another bird. Its presence indicates to a game bird that sees it that food is below and the area is safe to feed in. Swans, gulls, crows and herons are good examples of confidence decoys. Their use on or near a duck blind conveys a sense that nothing is amiss below.

CRAZING—This is a term applied to paint that has cracked in a manner that looks somewhat like a mosaic. Very characteristic of old paint.

DOVE TAIL—See "INLETTED"

EYES—The method a maker used to represent eyes on the decoys varied considerably and, in some cases, can be indicative of the maker or the school from which the decoys came. They used glass eyes that were either imported taxidermy eyes or simply the hat pins so popular with the ladies of those days. Sometimes thay merely painted the eye on or carved it right into the head. Upholstery tacks, screws, and even .22 caliber shell cases sometimes were used.

FLAT BOTTOM—Exactly as the name implies, this term refers to the bottom of a decoy that has a uniformly flat bottom. See "V-BOTTOM" and "ROUND BOTTOM."

GUNNING SCOW—This was a special sail boat rigged out with hoists and other necessary equipment for deploying the sink box or battery boats. There were three rather famous ones plying the Chesapeake Bay, **The Susquehanna, The North Carolina**, and **The Reckless**. See section on "BRANDS," pages 16 through 22, "PUNT GUN" and "SINK BOX."

HAWK WATCHING—A term describing the head and neck position of a decoy; up and wary.

HOLLOW BODY—Describes the fact that the decoy body is hollowed out. Generally the hollow-bodied decoys are of two-piece construction, but can be three or more.

IN USE REPAINT—See "REPAINT"

INLETTED—This usually refers to a specific method of attaching a head to a decoy body. It is accomplished by the carver fashioning a hole or cavity in the appropriate area of the body and carving the base of the head or neck portion to fit into this receptacle precisely. This renders the decoy much stronger and makes it more resistant to breakage by the natural tendency of many users to pick up the decoy by the head. Although used to a much lesser extent, the method is also occasionally found used to attach wings, bills, and sometimes other parts of a decoy. Use of this construction technique can help to determine the carver or school from which the decoy came. This inletting is usually a modification of a carpenter's mortise and tenon or dove tail joint.

KEEL—Just as in a boat a keel gave the decoy both upright and lateral stability. They were placed on decoys mainly in areas where the waters tended to be rougher than usual, but not limited to those areas by any means. Keels come in all shapes and materials. Most were fashioned as you would expect, of a strip of wood of varying depths placed longitudinally along the bottom of the decoy. The material and style can vary widely, however. There are fixed keels, swinging keels, folding keels, etc., and they can also be a combination of keel and ballast made of metal and/or wood. See "BALLAST."

LOW HEAD—A self-descriptive term describing decoys with little or no neck. The head is either very low or even almost tucked down into the top of the breast.

MARKET GUNNER—The market gunner was a hunter who made his living killing wildfowl for sale at market. For a detailed description of these men and their equipment, read pages 3 through 4 and see "SINKBOX" and "PUNT GUN."

MORTISED—See "INLETTED."

NAIL—A small protrusion situated at the front and top of the tip of the upper mandible or bill of some species of birds.

NARES or NOSTRILS—These are holes, one on either side of the upper mandibles. Some makers represented them with carving, others with paint or not at all, Occasionally the way a maker carves or paints these feathers is an identifying characteristic.

NECK NOTCH—A term describing a carved depression in the body of a decoy just behind the neck.

PLATE 2. Neck notch or thumbprint carving is evident just behind the head.

9

O.P.—See "ORIGINAL PAINT."

ORIGINAL PAINT [sometimes abbreviated O.P.]—This refers to a decoy which has the first or original paint that was applied by the maker. The term does not, however, appropriately describe a decoy that has been repainted by its original maker. See "REPAINT."

OVERSIZE—Refers to a decoy having been made in a scale larger than the normal size associated with the species of bird being carved.

PADDLE TAIL—A tail carved in a paddle shape, usually protruding from about the center of the rear end of the body.

PUNT GUN—Also called "Battery Guns," these were the guns used by the market hunters. These formidable guns could kill many, many birds with one shot. A typical punt gun would be twelve feet in overall length with an eight-foot barrel with a 1½ to 2 inch bore and weighing 100 to 125 pounds. They were capable of firing a whole pound of shot at once. Some were even bigger, being double-barrelled.

RAISED WING CARVING—Some decoy makers took pains to carve the body with the wings clearly raised slightly from the body. Typical of pre-1915 decoys by Elmer Crowell. Sometimes called simply "wing carving."

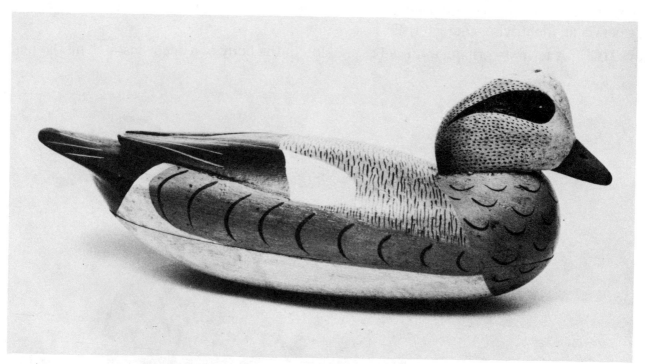

PLATE 3. This Delaware River School drake Widgeon decoy is an excellent example of "Raised Wing Carving."

RECENT REPAINT—See "REPAINT" below.

RE-HEAD—Because the head is the most vulnerable part of a decoy it is the part most usually damaged. So you can readily see that there can be many decoy bodies with heads from another decoy. These are called Re-heads.

REPAINT—There are really three different types of repainted decoys: (1) a repaint done by the original maker, (2) a repaint done by the owner and (3) a repaint done by a professional restorer. Although far the most desirable repainted decoy is one which has been repainted by the original maker, even it is less desirable than a decoy with the original or first painting by its maker. The user or owner repaint (other than the maker/user) is called a Working Repaint or In-use Repaint and is the most common condition an old decoy is found in. The third type, the restorer's work, is strictly a matter of owner or potential buyer preference.

RIG—A word used to describe a group of working decoys. The decoys you hunt with are your "rig" of decoys.

RIGGING—This is used to describe everything from the line tie and anchor line down to the anchor.

ROOTHEAD—This is appropriately used to describe decoys with heads made out of a root. Most of the roots were embellished by carving and/or painting, but some were used as is because of natural resemblance to the bird's head.

ROUND BOTTOM—A decoy with a rounded bottom as opposed to a "V-bottom" or "flat bottom," etc., is described as "round-bottomed."

SCHOOL—This is a broad term describing a group of decoy makers whose products share some common characteristics. Almost always a school of makers is also a certain geographical area in which they lived and worked. Their decoys were certainly influenced by the condition under which they were used, materials readily available, and last but not least individual makers' influence on each others products. A strict boundary delineating each school of makers is not possible to define. The schools overlap for the waters they hunted and the birds hunted tended to blend slowly from one type to another within the flyways.

SCRATCH FEATHER PAINTING—This is a method of feather painting where the maker lets the paint dry somewhat, then come back and scratches a feather pattern into the partially dry paint. This gives a very realistic texture to the finish.

SCULL BOAT—The scull boat was used all along the Eastern Seaboard from Maine all the way down through the Virginia Eastern Shore. The boat was used to hunt in the following manner: The hunter would deploy his rig of decoys in a likely spot and back off as much as a quarter of a mile and wait for the quarry to spot the rig and land. The boat made a slow, silent approach by sculling with a single oar over the stern of the boat and then they fired on their quarry.

SHADOW DECOY—This is a two-dimensional decoy such as a silhouette cut from a plank. Some of them have a bit of three-dimensional carving. The latter appears mostly in head carving. Shadow decoys usually come in one of three forms. One is used as a stick-up; another, sometimes called "Double Shadows," usually consists of two silhouettes fastened on either end of a couple of strips of wood with six more in various positions nesting in between. The third is illustrated in PLATE 4 on following page.

SHELF or SHELF CARVING—This term refers to a style or characteristic construction wherein the body is carved with a definite rise, making a portion of the bird's neck to receive the head, or head and neck, portion. See PLATE 5, following page.

PLATE 4. Shadow or silhouette decoys. Note the single point swivel attachment allowing them to be folded for ease of transport.

PLATE 5. This William T. Shaw drake Pintail from the Illinois River school illustrates the carved shelf made to receive the head and neck.

SILHOUETTE DECOY—See "SHADOW DECOY"

SINK BOX—Also known sometimes as "batteries" or "Battery Boats." These were used extensively by market gunners in the Atlantic Flyway, particularly in, but not limited to, the Chesapeake Bay area. They were usually one-man, narrow wooden boats with very narrow decks and "wings" of wood or canvas stretched on frames that extended the decks all around. On these wings were placed "Wing Ducks" fastened to the deck for both ballast and decoy. The hunter would frequently deploy a 500 to 600 rig of decoys.

The sink box along with the hunter and his gear was deployed by sailboats rigged for this specific purpose. They were called "gunning scows."

SLAT BODY—A type of decoy construction that utilizes wood slats bent over a frame. This lightweight construction was usually employed in the making of large decoys. Some decoys are commonly found with one slat bodies.

SLEEPER—A decoy carved in such a way as to represent a sleeping bird. Sometimes inaccurately called a confidence decoy. See CONFIDENCE DECOY.

SNEAK BOX—Usually associated with the Barnegat Bay area of New Jersey. This long, fairly narrow boat was completely decked over with only a small cockpit for the hunter. It was used extensively in the area. Lightweight in construction with a very shallow draft, it didn't have much weight capacity. This latter factor is said to have influenced the high development of hollow body decoys from that area; ostensibly developed to allow the hunter to carry many more in the sneak box than if they had been made with solid bodies. When the market gunner returned from his hunt he would often have bagged over a hundred ducks.

SOLID BODY—Refers to construction of a decoy body from solid wood as opposed to a hollow body. Generally the solid body will consist of one piece of wood, but they have been found also made of two, three or more laminated layers of wood.

SPLIT TAIL—Some decoy makers carved their decoys more realistically than others. This term refers to the differentiated carving of the tail feathers, showing as definite upper and lower sections. Generally associated with the Delaware River school.

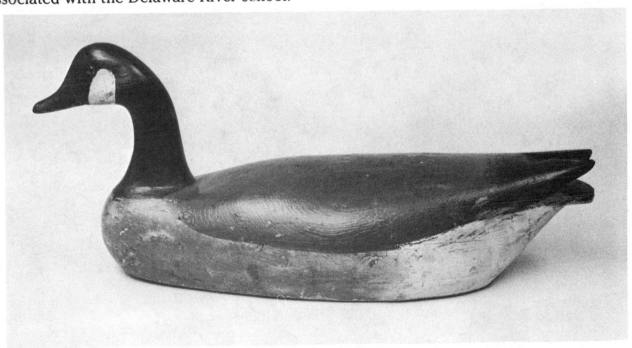

PLATE 6. This Delaware River Canada Goose decoy made by M. L. Perkins illustrates the Split-Tail carving. It could also be described as raised wing carving though this would not be entirely accurate. See "Raised Wing Carving."

13

STICK-UP—Frequently a decoy was made and mounted to one or more sticks or dowels representing legs (sometimes) that allowed the hunter to stick them into the ground or the bottom of a shallow or marshy area. There have been stick-ups of many species found, but the greatest majority are of shore birds.

STOOL—Once commonly used to describe a single decoy or a rig of decoys. The theory is that the word is derived from the European practice of fastening a live bird, usually a pigeon, to a movable pole or perch called a "stool." One can readily surmise that this also probably gave rise to the phrase "stool pigeon."

STOOLIES—Used to describe dead birds used as decoys.

THUMBPRINT CARVING—See "NECK NOTCH"

V-BOTTOM—Refers to the bottom of a decoy being in a "V" shape, when viewed form front or rear. See "FLAT BOTTOM" and "ROUND BOTTOM."

WATERLINE—A term utilized in describing where the joining of the upper and lower portions of a two-piece construction decoy is located; i.e., "above the waterline" or "below the waterline." The waterline itself is the level at which the decoy floats.

WING CARVING—See "RAISED WING CARVING."

WING DECOY—Usually made of cast iron or lead, these birds were made to serve a special purpose. They were made for use with the Sink Box or Battery Boats utilized by the market gunners as a means of balancing the boat and helping to camouflage the boat by lowering it in the water so that it presented a lower profile. They weighed anywhere from 8 to 40 pounds each, but there have been some found weighing much more. Some were made of wood but they are rarely found. Basically the wooden wing decoy was the upper one-half of a decoy. Some were easily convertible to a regular working decoy by adding an appropriate lower body piece. It can be assumed that this conversion accounts for their short supply. These conversions can be difficult to detect for there were many decoys made two or three-piece body construction. See "SINK BOX."

PLATE 7. A cast iron Canvasback wing duck.

WORKING REPAINT—See "REPAINT."

14

COLLECTING DECOYS

The successful and satisfying collecting of anything is not possible without careful study of what you collect, not to mention the possibility of making costly mistakes through ignorance. This book can no more provide you with all you need to know than a hunter can down every bird that passes through his sights, but it can help you get started. The following pages will give you needed information and directions toward a logical learning process.

Any collector who is serious about his particular interest will amass all that is written about it. To this end you will find later on a listing of other books that you need to begin obtaining for your collecting library. In addition to that will be a list of dealers and auction companies that sepcialize in or at least have moderate selections of decoys for sale.

IDENTIFICATION OF ANTIQUE DECOYS

There are many, many characteristics of decoys that make identification fairly easy in some cases. A considerable number of decoys, for instance, can be identified as to maker by such a simple things as the brands, logo, name or initials. Many makers can be determined because of a certain style or shape. Many of these early craftsmen had very significant styles of carving, construction technique or painting that were unique to the individual maker, making a decoy unmistakably his even in the absence of other identifying marks. This is also true of some of the factory produced birds. For instance some maker's decoys are all of the same distinctive body shape, only painted differently to represent different species of wildfowl. Others had a distinctive style of carving details such as carved delineation of the mandibles and/or carving separating them from the head of the bird. Others used the two-piece hollow construction exclusively or all with heads inletted or all with the upper and lower hollowed-out pieces joined, always above or always below the waterline.

The same type characteristics can be used to at least allow the collector to determine the school or area of the maker most of the time. The list goes on and on, paint styles, painting techniques, method of attaching head to body, position of head, species of bird carved, type of wood used, body shape, size of the decoy, eye types, and shaping of the tail and face carving, etc.

Certain designs are obviously meant to be used in shallow marshes while others are obviously made to be used in deep waters subject to weather.

Knowledge of changing migratory patterns can be helpful also. For instance, if you know that there were few or no Canada geese migrating through the Chesapeake Bay area prior to the 1930's, then you know any Canada goose decoy represented as being from there and dated by the seller as being made by a carver earlier than that is a case of mistaken identification. There would obviously not be any reason for such a decoy to have been made in that area at that time.

This general discussion may lead you to believe it is easy to date and identify the maker of any decoy; not so. True, there are some that are easy to spot and with time and experience gained from the easier identifications you can develop your ability to include identification of more, less obvious examples. The problem is that there are many types of decoy construction as there are opinions of just what constitutes an effective decoy. For the most part, luckily, carvers within a particular school were influenced by the species of bird hunted in his region and by the local conditions under which they had to be hunted. Therefore there **are** common characteristics. The discussion with each school will point these things out. To understand these discussions you must familiarize yourself with the Dictionary of Terminology in the previous pages. I suggest that, if you haven't already, you read through it and then each time you encounter a word or term you don't understand, refer back to the dictionary. This way you should end up with a working knowledge of most of the terms common to collecting decoys.

If you are a beginning collector you shouldn't be afraid of what you will find. There seems to be a tendency among novice collectors to pick up what is truly a fine decoy that has no documentation or provenance, in a shop or fleamarket, and then let it go. This reluctance is understandable, but if it has the look and feel of a good piece, by all means buy it. Many have an inherent ability to recognize good form and design. If you don't have it, you can develop it simply by handling and examining a few that are known quantities. You can sometimes be fooled, but not often, by today's decorative reproductions. More about this will be covered later.

BRANDS

The term "brand" as used in this book, and by most collectors, encompasses just about any markings placed on a decoy (usually on the bottom) by a user, maker or collector.

If a collector places his mark on a decoy it is usually a paper label or a rubber stamp type. There is seldom any doubt as to their marks. This practice is not particularly widespread for just about every good decoy, especially those that are extremely valuable, is known by more than one collector. Each decoy can usually be identified by its own distinctive nicks or wear pattern. Additionally, most of these high-value decoys are documented through auction catalog photography and description.

The remaining two categories of brands must be treated separately. User and maker brands can be very significant in dating a decoy, documenting its maker and influencing its value.

Unfortunately the majority of decoys don't have brands or, at the least, the brand doesn't mean anything. The latter is particularly true in the case of user brands unless the user can be identified and is of historical importance to collectors.

In the case of a decoy on which both user and maker brands appear, each being known and important, you have a real prize. The importance of either or both brands can have a very positive influence on the value of the decoy, especially of the decoy is otherwise insignificant. The value can be increased by two to five times, depending on the brand.

Any type of brand can be confusing to the uninitiated. To them any name found on the bottom of a decoy is thought to be that of the maker. More than once has someone thought that the name on the decoy that "Gramps" used was that of a friend or a hunting buddy who made it. Dealers are confronted with this from time to time.

What follow here are descriptions of some of the most famous and significant maker and user brands that you might find. There are, of course, more than are listed here, but the two lists are of many of those considered most important.

USER BRANDS

A user or owner brand can be that of the individual owner or of a hunting club or lodge. It usually appears in the form of a genuine brand such as those used in the cattle business. It wasn't a particularly expensive proposition in those days to have a local blacksmith fashion a branding iron for the impression of initials or name into a wooden decoy by heated iron or by striking with a hammer. Many owners and makers didn't go to the trouble but simply carved or painted their marks.

From time to time there may be more than one user brand found on a decoy. Whatever the number found, they can be interesting if not significant. For instance, I have seen a Harry Shourds Black Duck decoy with three brands on the bottom: H. W. Cain, B C P, A C. Now the "C" common to all three brands suggest that H.W. might be Grampa, A C might be his son, and B C P could be his grandson. Conjecture, yes, but if so think how exciting it might be for his family to possess this particular bird. Incidentally, this particular decoy was spotted by a collector in someone's front yard being used as a decoration with a heavy coat of chartreuse green. (More about decoys painted like this later.)

ACCOMAC was the name of a hunting club in the heart of the Virginia Eastern Shore about 65 miles north of Norfolk. This brand is found mostly on shore birds but also on a lot of good duck decoys. A decoy valued at about $200.00 would bring upwards of $850.00 if the Accomac brand were present.

BARRON is a relatively scarce brand to be found. It is the name of an Eastern Shore Virginia hunting club. It seems that the Barron hunters believed faithfully in the Mason factory-made decoys for as far as it is known so far the brand has shown up mostly on Mason decoys, but there have been a few very fine, unidentified decoys found bearing the brand as well. The Barron brand on a Mason decoy increases its value by about 50%. When it is present it is usually found in two places, on the back and on the side.

CHATEAU. Fred Chateau was a game warden who lived in Accord, Massachuetts. His brand has shown up on Joe Lincolns and some Martha's Vineyard decoys as well as a good many other New England decoys.

GOOSEVILLE G.C. The Gooseville Gunning Club was another Eastern Shore Virginia club. It went out of existence prior to World War I, so any bird found with this brand can be dated no later than 1917. Most decoys found bearing this brand will bring about twice the normal price for it.

HARD. This Hard Gun Club brand is found on many good factory decoys such as Masons, Dodge and Petersons.

NORTH CAROLINA. The **North Carolina** was one of three well known gunning scows. Each of the sailboat's rig of decoys was branded with the boat's name. As in the case of the other two gunning scows, just about any decoy with the brand would be worth at least $500.00. The **North Carolina** sank in 1888 on the Chesapeake Bay.

N P W. The initials in this brand are those of Nelson Price Whittaker. He was one of those who cast the heavy iron wing decoys for use with sink boxes.

ED PARSONS. Parsons was a legendary market gunner who hunted **only** over decoys made by Ben Dye and Captain John "Daddy" Holly; therefore, if you find a Parsons brand on a bird it is most likely to be one or the other. The brand was a "P" within a circle.

RECKLESS. The **Reckless** was one of the earliest gunning scows. The brand could make an otherwise insignificant upper Chesapeake Bay canvasback duck decoy in the $50 to $100 range worth $500 easily.

SUSQUEHANNA. The **Susquehanna** was another of the old gunning scows whose brand makes the decoy worth much more than the norm. Same comments apply here as to the **Reckless** and the **North Carolina**. The **Susquehanna** sank just before the Civil War so, obviously, and decoy branded with its name pre-dates 1860-65.

SUYDAM. This brand belonged to a wealthy Long Island family that did much sport hunting in Long Island Sound. The brand shows up relatively often on good Long Island decoys.

PLATE 8.

MAKER BRANDS

Few of the probably thousands of individuals who carved decoys for personal or commercial purposes identified them with a brand of some sort, but most of the factory-made decoys did carry brands. The factory brands will be covered separately in that section of the book. The listing presented here is of several of the more important makers who sometimes, often, or always identified their decoys with a brand.

The descriptions below are of brands only. The individual characteristics of the carver's products are discussed in the text of the school of carvers he is normally associated with.

MAKER BRANDS (Non-Factory) of Significance

Joel Barber. This is the same Joel Barber we have discussed earlier. He is one of the big names in decoy collecting. After Barber wrote his book **Wild Fowl Decoys** he decided he would try his hand at carving decoys himself. His brand, when present, is very distinctive and readily recognizable. It is represented in PLATE 9 on the following page.

PLATE 9.

PLATE 10. This Redhead made by Joel Barber is branded. It has been said that he once stated that he didn't place the brand (Plate 9) on but eight of his decoys. This bird was made only as an example of what he thought a "modern" (1934) decoy ought to look like.

PLATE 11. A Joel Barber Ring Neck drake made for use as a working decoy. Most of his decoys were made for the aesthetics rather than the utility. This particular decoy was supposedly made for use. Its condition testifies that if it ever was used to hunt over it was well cared for. It bears his hand signature on the bottom where the keel has been removed.

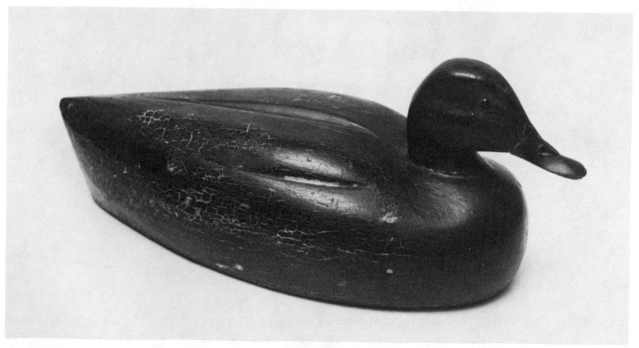

PLATE 12. A Joel Barber Black Duck made very much like a St. Clair Flats decoy with a hollow body and a one-quarter inch bottom board.

Thomas B. Chambers was a carver from the St. Clair Flats area. He did not always place his brand but when he did it is easily to identify. It simply stated "Thomas B. Chambers, Maker" and was stenciled onto the bottom.

Nathan Cobb Family. The Cobb family were originally New Englanders who migrated south to Virginia. Their products are best identified by construction techniques and style, but they sometimes carved their initials into the bird. Since they did not brand but carved an initial into their decoys, it is more a matter of interest than anything else. Most of the time you will find only an "N" for Nathan Cobb, an "E" or an "A" carved into their products, if you find any at all. Both are illustrated in Plates 13 and 14.

PLATE 13.

PLATE 14.

21

Elmer Crowell. The oval brand was customarily used by Crowell starting around 1915 and the rectangular version is usually associated with his later work and/or his son Kleon's work. Unfortunately the decoys carved by Crowell prior to 1915 before he adopted a brand are considered to be his finest work. Collectors should be aware that a few decoys have shown up with an apparently authentic Crowell brand which are known not to be his work.

Lee and Lem Dudley were twins who lived, hunted and carved decoys in the far northern Currituck Sound area of the outer banks of North Carolina. The brand "L.D." found on their decoys could be either brother, although the late Bill Mackey states in his **American Bird Decoys** that most probably it was Lem Dudley who carved most of the decoys. Simplest of the brands to forge, it has been known to happen so it behooves any collector interested in Dudley decoys to get to know their characteristics intimately. Illustrated in Plate 115.

Mitchell Fulcher was also a North Carolina maker. He, like the Dudleys, also identified his decoys with his initials, "M.F."

Laing. Albert Laing decoys are almost always found with his last name branded large and clear on the bottom.

DECORATIVE AND REPRODUCTION DECOYS

A discussion of decorative decoys of the several available types is absolutely necessary in a book devoted to guiding the collector in this hobby. Experienced and seasoned collectors are quite cognizant of these products, but some could very well mislead those who are new to the hobby or at least contemplating beginning a collection of decoys.

Collectively, decorative decoys comprise several types. These are:

(1) Those decoys being carved and painted by craftsman/artists of great talent. They could be called "Modern Folk Artists."

(2) Reproductions of classic antique decoys. These are almost always offered in a reduced scale from the originals. Some are offered in a "limited edition" and all are (or should be) well identified as to exactly what they are.

(3) Those decoys factory-made or hand-made that are offered to the public strictly as a decorator item. They have no claim, nor do their makers make any claim, to anything other than that.

(4) Those decoys offered by various companies in kit form for finishing by individual hobbyists or those that are made by individuals for their own use or enjoyment.

The first category is the most important of the four mentioned above. The carvers of these fine bird sculptures, for that is truly what they are, find their progenitors among the early master makers of the working wildfowl decoy. Many of those early makers just weren't satisfied with their product unless it reflected their own high knowledge of the anatomy and habit of the living bird. They were truly artists who couldn't help expressing their talents in the working decoy.

The contemporary carvers are carrying on the active pursuit of this acknowledged original early American Folk Art. It could be said that the competition of today finds its roots in the first organized competition of decoy makers that was held in Bell Port, Long Island, in 1913. Charles E. "Shang" Wheeler, one of the old master decoy makers, entered his work in this competition and walked away The Grand Champion.

Most of these contemporary sculptures in wood are easily recognized by their extreme detail and excellent workmanship. In addition to this attention to anatomical and feather detail, the decoy must also pass a set of strict requirement of floating attitude, etc., taken from both the real birds' habits and those that would be necessary for a working decoy.

A few contemporary carvers do work in the old style as in the accompanying photographic plates.

The second group, that of reproductions, is probably the most controversial among collectors. Many seasoned serious collectors look upon these products with disdain, but the fact remains that they exist and satisfy the appetites of many individuals. They are usually done in a smaller scale than the original and well marked as reproductions. Some are machine made and some entirely hand-made. Like the originals, however, even the machine made likenesses have to have finishing, carving and painting applied by hand.

Third is a group of decoys that are factory-made or hand-made for decorative purposes only. The legitimate makers of these decorator items clearly mark their products so that the new collector should have no problem identifying them for what they are. Some are strikingly beautiful and can make wonderful additions to those who decorate their houses with early American style furnishings.

The last category is that of the various individual wood-working hobbyists who either create their own designs or finish factory-made kits that are available in various stages of completion. The finished products in this category can vary from crude to wonderfully detailed decorations depending on the abilities of the hobbyist.

PLATE 16. A drake Merganser made by contemporary carver Dave B. Hawthorne of Salisbury, Maryland.

PLATE 17. Hen Widgeon by contemporary maker Frank Beck of New Holland, Pennsylvania.

PLATE 18. Drake Widgeon mate to the Frank Beck hen.

In the first edition of this book I stated that it wasn't unreasonable to assume that there may be some hunters out there who still carve their own working decoys from wood simply for the sheer satisfaction of making their own wooden working decoys in the tradition of their ancestors. Well, not only did I find that to be true, but was made a gift of a handsome wood duck decoy made by a Canadian hunter, Bev Doolittle. In an accompanying note he said he made and hunted over his own rigs.

All the above have a particular market, from the active collector of the beautiful decoys created by contemporary artisans to the kits and individually made decorative decoy. They are not, however, looked upon as a part of decoy collecting. The information is presented more for interest and especially for the neophyte collector so that he may not become confused in the early phases of building a collection and learning about antique decoys.

MISREPRESENTATIONS, FORGERIES AND FAKES

In the course of research for this book I thought it might be interesting if I were to take a day's tour through my own area to see what, if anything, I might turn up in the way of old decoys. I found many types of decorative decoys, all priced fairly reasonably for what they were, one identifiable, rather inferior but decidedly old decoy priced at $80.00, and the last one I found was the most interesting; that is, from the standpoint of what the new collector might occasionally run into. It was a nicely formed and carved decoy with lots of "documentation." There was a large tag attached to it giving its maker's name (unknown to me), its origin (Long Island, New York), dates, etc. The body was graceful and carved nicely but it was battered beyond help. There was also a price tag attached to the neck by a string-$145.00! What makes this so incredible is that the neck and head were made of **plastic**, not to mention the fact that it was in a much-too-large scale for the body. I have no doubt that this antique shop owner accepted the bird in good faith from someone else. It was not **intentionally** misrepresented, but it was nevertheless a misrepresentation. I have no doubt that even the newest "wet-behind-the-ears" collector of old wooden decoys would not likely be taken in by this, but it serves well enough to illustrate a point. You need to study and handle the "real McCoy" before leaping into collecting. It isn't hard nor is it a frightening proposition to learn how to recognize a good vs. a bad decoy in this type of encounter. It is the outright fake or forgery that you need to be aware of.

Fortunately there are few if any nefarious dealers in antique decoys and most antique shop owners and fleamarketeers are honest. The latter two, however, seldom know decoys. These shops and fleamarkets can be good hunting grounds if you know your stuff. You might find a real treasure for just a few bucks.

Using the example of the plastic head above, we come to the problems of "reheads." Don't misunderstand reheads as misrepresentations, fakes or forgeries because the discussion appears here. The majority of old bodies fitted with old heads that are not the originals are legitimate. Remember that bills and heads are usually the part of a decoy most susceptible to damage in handling, so many hunters had to replace heads from time to time. Don't worry about that problem for now. The ability to recognize a rehead most of the time will come with increased familiarity with individual, recognizable characteristics of various makers. Reheads represent an altered form of a decoy, hence its inclusion here.

So far not too many outright fakes or forgeries have reared their ugly heads, but it has happened. A few obviously inferior decoys have been found with the easily recognizable oval brand of Elmer Crowell, and the most popular forged "brand" is that of Lee and Lem Dudley for they simply carved "L.D." into their products. Fakes of Mason decoys have shown up and by far the most popular subjects of forgers are the decoys made by the Ward brothers, Lem and Steve.

So far, so good. Not many of these bogus offerings have turned up but, as in any area of collecting where some of the items have reached values as high as decoys have, we have to be ready for anything. There are many, many exceptionally talented craftsman in the United States today and it would be safe to say that among them are a few bad apples. In addition, with the spate of well formed decorator decoy bodies and kits for the hobbyist, a dishonest individual wouldn't have to be necessarily endowed with great carving talent, only a degree of ingenuity.

There are many ways to artifically age a paint finish; for instance, I know from experience that it can be done fairly effectively. In the course of preparation for my book **Old Fishing Lures and Tackle** I reproduced a couple of classic bass plugs in my workshop, painted them and "aged" the paint. They would never fool a knowledgeable collector, by the neophyte **might** be taken in by my product. Incidentally, I clearly identified these plugs as to what they were and they have never left my possession. To be on the safe side I am in the process of repainting them with a shiny new paint job so I can fish them.

Another potential problem is the proliferation, over the past few years, of very fine looking contemporary hand-carved or machine made decoys that are rendered in the style of the old master carvers. Most of these, fortunately, are blends of several styles or just simply a talented designer's own creation and are marked in such a way as to identify them as modern. The problem is some of them are not so marked and others are actual copies not marked as such. Most really experienced collectors and sellers can readily identify these as bogus, but those of us a little less punctilious might be fooled.

All of this comes down to one cardinal rule of collecting: Establish a good working relationship with one or more recognized, knowledgeable and trustworthy dealers. I know of none of these dealers who wouldn't back up his sale to you with a guarantee of reimbursement if what he sold you turns out to be other than what he represented the decoy as.

RESTORATION AND REPAIRS

There are always two schools of thought among collectors when the subject of restoration comes up. One is well-labelled the purist approach; that is the strong belief that the decoy should be left "as is," that no restoration effort should be made. Some collectors of this persuasion will, however, approve of taking the years of working repaints down to what is left of the first or original coat. I am of the purist persuasion but would, in the case of my own collection, be among those who would like to take any crude repaints down to the first or second coat, especially in the case of the Harry Shourds black duck discussed on page 69.

The other group are those who advocate complete or partial restoration. This could run the spectrum actually from a simple paint touch-up to replacing broken or rotten wood parts and faithfully reproducing the style of painting of the original maker.

What you do or think about restoration is strictly a personal decision made under whatever circumstances there are. You should know, however, that probably the majority of serious collectors prefer the decoy to be left as it is. Further, if you do elect to have a decoy restored, it is incumbent upon you to be certain that you say it has been done before selling or swapping the bird. My own opinion goes a step further. Each restored decoy should be clearly and permanently marked as such in an inconspicuous place, preferably on the bottom. That way all subsequent owners will know exactly what has been done to it.

The condition of a decoy is an extremely important consideration when placing a value on it. A restoration of any sort can have a tremendous influence on its value in either direction, so you must think carefully before having any restoration done.

VALUE DETERMINATION

The condition of a decoy can be an extremely important consideration when placing a value on it. A restoration of any sort can have a tremendous influence on its value in either direction, so you must think carefully before having any restoration done.

There is presently some controversy brewing, with regard to restoring and repairing decoys. While it is easy to be purist and collect only those examples that are in what could be called "mint" condition one would find his collection rather limited by the rarity of such examples, not to mention expensive. Such examples could command rather daunting prices. The controversy revolves around the value of restored or repaired decoys. Some collectors feel that a beautifully restored decoy should be worth nearly, if not as much as a pristine example while others argue that they should be considerably devalued. This is not a problem with any real solution that would cover all cases. It must of necessity, be a subjective decision and one which must be made personally by each collector.

How could you possibly make a sweeping statement covering all cases? How could you, for example, say that an Ira Hudson decoy restored to perfect condition be worth as much as one that is just as nice that had never been damaged at all? Hudson produced a prodigious number of decoys in his career and there are plenty of nice examples out there. There are other makers, such as Shang Wheeler who made fine decoys, but in limited numbers. In that case the restored one could conceivably be valued at near or the same as an undamaged one.

Some years ago, as guest columnist in Alan Haid's column **DECOYS** in *Sporting Classics* magazine*, Hal Sorenson set forth an excellent criteria for evaluating decoys as to condition. I could certainly do not better, so with the kind permission of the magazine the following reprint is presented for your use.

SOME MAJOR FACTORS THAT DETERMINE THE VALUE OF OLD DECOYS

by Hal Sorenson

Unlike the rather precise determinants of value assigned to individual stamps, coins, and other collectible items, one must contend with many variables when assessing old decoys. Five collectors could easily look at one decoy and come up with five different appraisals. In judging the general value of one decoy over another, the folowing major factors must be taken into consideration.

RARITY: The number of examples in existence of a particular species by a particular maker. How many or few examples constitute "rare" is difficult to discern. Usually the price assigned to a decoy by a knowledgeable seller is a good indicator of how unique the example is.

MAKER: The relative importance of a carver's name, whether an individual or a factory, will have considerable bearing on the value of a decoy. For instance, with two different but equally handsome old redhead drakes in similar condition, one by a "name" maker and the other by "maker unknown," the "name maker" decoy will undoubtedly command the higher price. The work of a "name maker" will also be worth more to a collector who specializes in that maker's decoys or who specializes in decoys from that region. However, many "known" carvers are not "name" carvers regardless of how many birds they may have produced. Collectors and publicity determine who is and who is not recognized as a "name" carver.

CONDITION: In the case of an old decoy, the word "condition" applies both to the physical appearance of the decoy and the painting. A Shourds merganser in fine original paint, but with the bill broken off and a large gouge in one side would be comparable in condition to the same style decoy in near perfect physical state but with 90% of the original paint worn off, or the same decoy having been repainted.

Collectors vary in their interpretation of word like "excellent," "very good," "fair," etc. The break down between categories should be considered a general guideline.

Mint: 100% perfect, original condition. A decoy in mint condition would generally be unused.

Excellent: Near mint, with minor wear.

Very Good: At least 90% of the original paint still intact; probably has a few nicks and bruises. A repaired bill acceptable if not noticeable.

Good: Shows quite a bit of wear but still has 60-90% of the original paint left. Minor restoration such as bill repair and breast retouched acceptable.

Fair: In pretty rough shape and probably needs restoration to make it worthy of a spot on the collector's shelf.

*Pages 27 and 73 of Volume II, Issue VI, January/February 1984. Copyright 1984, *Sporting Classics* magazine.

Poor: Both body and paint in bad condition; perhaps major body cracks. A decoy in this condition is hardly worth picking up unless exceedingly rare.

Repainted: Whether an old or new paint job, it was probably done by someone other than the carver. Certain of todays decoy artists specialize in restoring old "name" decoys with a sincere effort to capture the appearance of the originals. Others will take any old block, good or bad, and repaint it in whatever pattern or colors they happen to feel like at the moment.

PHONIES, FAKES, COPIES, ETC.: A newly made decoy which appears to be an old original by a known maker; or a recently made decoy which looks old, but is unsigned or undated by the maker. Some fakes are so good they fool the experts! Study your proposed purchase carefully. Any honest dealer or collector will be glad to let you do so and most will give you a money-back guarantee. When in doubt, however, try to consult a third, knowledgeable party.

SPECIES AND SEX: These two factors affect price because certain species are much rarer than others and some species are more highly prized than others. In addition, both the old handcarvers and the factories produced far more drakes than hens. Drake wood duck decoys are very rare compared to most species; hen wood duck decoys are almost non-existent. Species such as merganser and teal have wide appeal. While both were produced in pretty fair quantity, collectors tend to snap them up and hang onto them, resulting in a relative shortage in the marketplace.

GRADE: Most factories and some individual carvers produced their decoys in two or more grades. The fancier the painting and the most detailed the carving, the higher the original selling price. In most cases, the same holds true when a collector goes to make a purchase today.

STYLE: Carving and painting patterns constitute "style." The Ward Bros, and the factory decoys made by Mason are two examples of those who produced a number of different styles-especially in carving pattern-over their many decoy-producing years. Collectors who study enough examples by a particular maker will be able to determine which of the styles he likes best.

AESTHETIC AND ARTISTIC PREFERENCES: Both of these factors are personal in nature except for certain "classics" agreed upon by the majority of decoy enthusiasts. Strip away a name, disregard rarity, species, etc., and one gets down to aesthetic consideration do you like the decoy or not? Disagreements in preference will most likely arise over the "primitives"—those decoys with no pedigree, which border on crude workmanship and yet have appeal from anesthetic and artistic viewpoints.

HISTORICAL ASSOCIATIONS: Some people put considerable value on who-shot-over-what-decoy. Unless the association is a personal one, I consider it immaterial whose hands previously held one of my pride-and-joys.

REGIONAL PREFERENCES: Because decoy styles vary from region to region, many collector prefer to specialize in decoys from a specific area, i.e., Delaware River, Cape Cod, Barnegat Bay, Chesapeake Bay, Illinois River, etc. As mentioned above, a person who specializes in a certain area is likely to place a higher value on decoys which originate from there.

AGE: All other factors considered, the actual age of a particular decoy is not very important. Take two similar decoys by the same maker: it matters not whether one is ten or even twenty years older that the other. From a collector's standpoint, it also makes little difference if a clunker was made in 1970 or 1900...it's still a clunker.

DECOYS IN UNUSUAL POSES: Sleeper, swimmers, feeders, preeners, callers and the like are rare in the overall decoy picture. As a result, this factor probably belongs under the rarity category. Such poses add interest to the decoy shelves and dollars to the value.

CARE OF YOUR COLLECTION

You might think that just because many of your decoys survived the ravages of water and rough treatment by hunters, you don't have to give them any special consideration in the display or transport of them. If you give it just a little thought, millions of decoys were made and used over the years. There can be no realistic estimate made as to how many have survived, but suffice it to say that they are becoming more and more difficult to find in any condition, much less good to excellent condition.

Any wooden object is subject to a number of different hazards. "Checking," the splitting or cracking of decoys is not an uncommon problem. Some of it is due to the maker not using sufficiently seasoned wood. Due to subsequent drying out of unseasoned wood, checking can and does happen. Consider also that a decoy may have lain untouched for years in a boathouse, shed or barn with more or less constant moisture conditions. You find it, add it to your collection in your modern climate-controlled home, which is very dry as a rule and after some months a crack appears. It could be dismaying, but you can do little about the problem unless you have the wherewithal to install expensive systems like the better museums have. This is a problem most of us will have to accept as inevitable. It doesn't happen often but does nevertheless happen.

There are some precautions you can take to at least retard this problem, and others you can take easily to alleviate the likelihood of damage.

For one thing, make sure that your display is not subjected to direct blasts of heat or cold from a floor or wall register. They look great on a mantel, but if you use your fireplace even just occasionally, don't leave them up there. That is one of the worst places to display them. Heat and smoke will do much harm to your decoys.

Never let them be exposed to direct sunlight even for a few minutes each day. The cumulative damaging effect of ultraviolet light from the sun can fade the already fragile paint. A little known fact is that continuous exposure to fluorescent light can do the same thing. Try to avoid exposure to either one.

There has been some controversy concerning applying oil or wax to a decoy. Once again a purist might not agree because it alters the original state of the decoy. Again this must be an individual decision, but it is known that proper application of these materials to any wood acts as a preservative by "feeding" the wood. You wouldn't hesitate to care for a piece of fine antique furniture in this manner, so why not your decoys? Obviously, rigorous rubbing of an already old and fragile paint job may do it irreversible harm. Judgement enters into the picture in this case.

Not too much has been written about termites, "powder-post" beetles or lyctid beetles and other wood boring insects, but this problem presents a very real and present danger. If they are in the wood, they can not only damage or destroy your decoy but can literally eat your house from around you if they spread to the wood surrounding the infested object.

If you find small piles of fine dust around a decoy, don't panic. Just remove it from your collection and isolate it. Recent research has indicated that freezing the piece of infested wood will usually kill the live lyctid beetles, but not much is yet known about the effect of the larvae of the beetle. My advice would be to freeze for several days and isolate it for about a month, preferably in a sealed plastic bag or tightly lidded metal box. Inspect it periodically for new evidence of the dust-like, powdery spills from the tiny holes made by the beetle. If no new ones are found, you're probably safe.

A most important consideration in the care of your collection is insurance and theft protection. This can be a paramount importance if your collection has grown for some years and represents a sizable sum of money in appreciated value. Additionally, much of it may be irreplaceable.

There are some safeguards against these threats, not the least of which is insurance. I would bet that a great many collectors are sublimely comforted by the mistaken belief that their homeowners' insurance covers their collection. They are suffering from a common but risky supposition. Most of these policies specifically exclude such collections. This is not the place to go into the complexities of special insurance riders or policies to cover a valuable collection. It does serve to give notice to the collector that the situation should be examined by a trusted insurance expert.

A careful record of your collection is almost obligatory in its protection. If you have a good record of the items in your collection, it can be of immeasurable aid in documenting your loss in the case of loss due to fire, theft, etc. Law enforcement authorities often turn up stolen goods that cannot be claimed by the true owner because of lack of ownership documentation.

As we have already noted, many decoys are documented through auction sales catalog photography and collector familiarity with certain of the more well-known examples. Collector George Ross Star Jr., M.D., in the "Wildfowl Decoys" chapter in **The American Sporting Collector's Handbook*** states on page 49, "Personally, I am always pleased with publication of photos of the better birds in my collection on the premise that the more people who can recognize them the harder it would be to sell any illegally and the more apt they are to be recognized and reported if offered for sale." I strongly agree with Dr. Starr, however caution should be exercised in your choice of publication, if the occasion arises. One collector I know of refuses to be identified as the owner of his birds when photographed for publication, for fear of burglary. This is sensible if he doesn't have a sophisticated and reliable security system for his collection.

It is strongly recommended that you accomplish a detailed listing of each decoy in your collection. A very effective method is to photograph each of them and record any distinguishing characteristics on the reverse of the photo, such as species, maker, marks or brands, size, and any readily recognizable wear patterns, nicks, etc. You should keep this in a safe place away from your home such as a bank safe deposit box. If you wish to have such a record in your home for the convenience of making changes and additions, make sure it is a **second** set and be certain that you make the same additions and corrections to the other set in your safe deposit box. With this kind of record, in the event of theft and recovery, you should have no problem reclaiming your decoys. It will also go a long way establishing the amount of your loss to insurance companies.

*Edited by Allan J. Liu, copyright 1976 by Winchester Press

DECOY DEALERS AND COLLECTORS

There are hundreds of collectors around the country some of which are dealers as well. The best way to make contact with many fellow collectors is to obtain a copy of the **National Directory of Decoy Collectors**, edited by Gene and Linda Kangas. You might find it available from a dealer, but you can get a copy direct from them if you wish. The address is 6852 Ravenna Road, Painesville, Ohio 44077.

Aside from the dealer source of decoys there are also the collectors. In the course of collecting decoys many of them will change their tastes or direction of their efforts or simply replace a decoy with another found in better condition. Whatever the reasons often collectors have a few birds they would like to sell or trade. Collectors with anything to sell will probably be glad to provide you with a list upon request. This is certainly true of dealers and for a nominal fee to cover printing and postage they will mail it to you. When writing for information to either group it is always advisable to include a self-addressed stamped envelope (SASE).

When contemplating a purchase it is always best to obtain as detailed a description as possible. Along with this information it is a great help to get a good quality photograph also. Obviously the best way to buy is on the spot after a careful personal examination, but there is no decoy supermarket around the corner from most of us so the mail and the telephone are what we have to use. If, after you have taken all the steps to insure what you are buying is what you get and when you get it it isn't, most dealers will back up their offerings if you can satisfy them that what you bought is not what you thought it was.

Once you have located a few folks you like to deal with hang on to them. Remember the old admonishment, "If you buy furs, know your furrier."

The following list of dealers are well established and have fine reputations. They are recommended as your first contacts when starting a collection of decoys.

Dick McIntyre
835 Bonita Drive
Fripp Island, South Carolina 29920

Bob Richardson
Box 433
Cambridge, Maryland 21613

Dan S. Young
Route 1, Box 52
Paradise Island
Awendaw, South Carolina 29429

John Delph
Riverswynd Antiques
465 Union Street
Marshfield, Massachusetts 02050

H.A. Fleckenstein Jr.
Box 279
East New Market, Maryland 21631

Hawthorne House
RFD 6, Box 409
Salisbury, Maryland 21801

Chares T. Ward
2486 Washington Ave.
Oceanside, L.I., New York 11572

Charles F. Murphy
The Sneak Box
Strawberry Banke
P.O. Box 4033
Portsmouth, New Hampshire 03801

Ted Harmon
2320 Main Street
Barnstable, Massachusetts 02630

DECOY AUCTIONS

There are many auctions of old decoys that take place each year in the United States. Most of them are smallish and are held in conjunction with the meetings of various collector organizations or wildfowl festivals, etc. Watch for the dates and places these take place in the publications aimed at decoy collectors and hunters.

There are, in addition to the meetings, some auction companies that devote varying degrees of attention to the auctioning of old American decoys. These companies are listed below along with their addresses. Attendance at these auctions can be an education in itself. It gives the collector a chance to personally examine and handle many different examples of decoys from the hands of dozens of makers representing most of the major schools of makers. You can experience the differences first hand. Another great benefit to be derived from these auction companies is to obtain the auction sales catalogs. The catalogs are heavily illustrated and serve very nicely as identification and documentation manuals for literally hundreds of decoys and related items. Be sure that you get a copy of every sales catalog that is issued by the auction companies whether you are interested in buying or not. Don't forget to include the extra buck or two so that they will send the results of the sale. This will give you a good reference as to value when you need it. These results may not reflect tha actual market as accurately as we would want it. Don't forget that the occasion of an auction can be influential on the buyers and actual prices realized can reflect the heat of the moment so to speak. "Auction fever" can do strange things. Keep in mind also that a collector may not be in hot pursuit of a particular decoy and be willing to pay a great deal more than the bird is worth, especially if he has any bidding competition from another collector who covets the same bird. What this means simply is that the results may not reflect the true picture, but it is just about all we have to go on. It's going to be a "ball park" figure and a good place to start.

All of the companies listed below are well known to collectors of just about anything. Each of them holds auctions for many things other than decoys. The reason they are singled out is that all of them do hold special auctions for the sale of old decoys in some quantity.

RICHARD A. BOURNE CO., INC.
P.O. Box 141
Hyannis Port, Massachusetts 02647

WILLIAM DOYLE GALLERIES
175 East 87th Street
New York, New York 10028

SOTHEBY'S
1334 York Avenue
New York, New York 10021

JAMES D. JULIA-GARY GUYETTE, INC.
RFD #1, Box 830
Fairfield, Maine 04937

RICHARD W. OLIVE
P.O. Box 337
Kennebunk, Maine 04043

PHILLIPS
867 Madison Avenue
New York, New York 10021

MIDWEST DECOY COLLECTORS ASSOCIATION

This is a not for profit, educational organization of collectors and lovers of decoys. As their 1991 directory states: "The purpose…is to seek out and preserve the old decoys, gather information about old carvers and their methods for historical records, and hold an annual show for decoy collectors and carvers for the exchange of information about their origin."

Don't let the name fool you into thinking it is for Midwest collectors only. The membership is almost 600 and they come from all over the United States and Canada. Membership is highly recommended, not only to support its goals, but to put you in touch with other collectors. This is easily undertaken through the annual directory of members. The dues are $15.00 a year. The address is 2172 Ferris Lane, St. Paul, MN 55113.

PERIODIC PUBLICATIONS FOR DECOY COLLECTORS

The following is a list of publications that are either devotes exclusively to collecting decoys or contain regularly running features or columns about decoys, their makers or related materials. All contain varying degrees of decoy sales advertising.

DECOY HUNTER

901 North 9th, Clinton, Indiana 47842. Subscription cost is $12.00 per year for six issues.

DECOY MAGAZINE

P.O. Box 1900, Montego Bay Station, Ocean City, Maryland 21842

NORTH AMERICAN DECOYS

Hillcrest Publications, Inc. P.O. Box 246, Spanish Fork, Utah 84660. This is a very high quality magazine that has varied quite a bit in frequency of publication over the years. There are no rates published for a subscription presently but it is highly recommended that the collector write them and have your name placed on their mailing list. There are some back issues available from them and well worth adding to your reference library.

SPORTING CLASSICS

P.O. Box 770, Camden, South Carolina 29020. Subscription cost is $12.00 per year for six issues. This fine magazine used to carry a regular column about old decoys and ocassionally runs features about decoys. Covers many different types of sporting collectibles as well.

WARD FOUNDATION NEWS

The Ward Foundation, Inc., Salisbury State College, Salisbury, Maryland 21801. This is a quarterly magazine published for the members of the foundation. Membership includes a subscription to the magazine.

RECOMMENDED BOOKS FOR DECOY COLLECTORS

To purchase all the books listed below would represent quite a sizable cash outlay, but each of them is a valuable tool in learning about decoys and their makers. If you collect from all the various schools of makers you will have to make an effort to obtain them all over time. Each of them has indispensable data for collectors. If you specialize in one or two areas you are a bit more fortunate, but even study of areas in which you do not collect can be very helpful. The study of the entire area of decoy collecting is a fascinating and enjoyable task. You may get lucky if you make a trip to your local library. There are, incidentally, some really good books about hunting and American folk art that have a good sections on old decoys so don't overlook them in the card catalog.

The list following contains many books that are out-of-print and no longer available from the publishers. There are, however, many book sellers who specialize in locating and obtaining out-of-print books. One of the biggest and most successful is the:

HIGHWOOD BOOKSHOP
P.O. Box 1246
Traverse City, Michigan 49685-1246
PHONE: (616) 271-3898

Owned and operated by Lou Razek, Highwood Bookshop specializes in new and old sporting books and periodicals. He stocks thousands of old periodicals and probably has the biggest stock of new and out-of-print decoy books in the country.

AMERICAN BIRD DECOYS from the collection of William J. Mackey, Jr. A catalog of a 1967 exhibit in St. Paul, Minnesota and Oshkosh, Wisconsin. Out of print.

AMERICAN BIRD DECOYS by William J. Mackey, Jr. Copyright 1965 by William J. Mackey, Jr. Originally published by E.P. Dutton and reissued by Schiffer Publishing Ltd. Various editions by Schiffer to 1985. Now out-of-print.

AMERICAN FACTORY DECOYS by Henry A. Fleckenstein, Jr. Copyright 1981 by Henry A. Fleckenstein, Jr. Schiffer Publishing Ltd., Box E, Exton, Pennsylvania 19431.

AMERICAN DECOYS FROM 1865 TO 1920 by Quintana Colio. Copyright 1972. Science Press. Out of print.

AMERCIAN SPORTING COLLECTORS HANDBOOK, edited by Allen J. Liu. Copyright 1976 by the Winchester Press. Out of print.

AMERICAN SPORTING COLLECTORS HANDBOOK, Revised Edition, edited by Allen J. Liu. Copyright 1982. Winchester Press. Out of print.

AMERICAN WILDFOWL DECOYS by Jeff Waingrow. Copyright 1985, E.P. Dutton. Reissued by Weathervane Books, 1989. Both editions out-of-print.

THE ART OF THE DECOY; AMERICAN BIRD CARVINGS by Adele Earnest. Originally published in 1965 by Crown Publishers, New York and Clarkson N. Potter, New York. Reissued in several editions and printing by various publishers. Present edition published 1981 by Schiffer Publishing Ltd., Box E. Exton, Pennsylvania 19341.

AUCTION CATALOG OF THE DR. GEORGE STARR COLLECTION. Issued 1986 by the Richard A. Bourne Company. Hard cover edition.

AUCTION CATALOGS, THE WILLIAM J. MACKEY COLLECTION-1973, 1974. A set of five catalogs issued by the Richard A. Bourne Company.

BARNEGAT BAY DECOYS AND GUNNING CLUBS by Patricia H. Burke. Copyright 1985. Ocean County Historical Society. Limited edition of 1000 soft cover copies. Now out-of-print.

BEN J. SCHMIDT-MICHIGAN CARVER by Lowell Jackson.

THE BIRD DECOY, AN AMERCIAN ART FORM by Paul A. Johnsgard. Copyright 1976. University of Nebraska Press.

CHESAPEAKE BAY DECOYS by R.H. Richardson. Copyright 1973. Crowhaven Publishers. Out of print.

CHINCOTEAGUE CARVERS AND THEIR DECOYS by Barry and Velma Berkey. Copyright 1977. Tidewater Publishers, P.O. Box 109, Cambridge, Maryland 21613.

THE COLLECTOR'S GUIDE TO DECOYS by Bob and Sharon Huxford. Copyright 1990, Schroeder Publishing Company. Collector Books, P.O. Box 3009, Paducah, Kentucky 42001. A compilation of major auction results for the four year period 1985-1989.

CONNECTICUT DECOYS, CARVERS AND GUNNERS by Henry C. Chitwood. Copyright 1987. Schiffer Publishing Ltd., Box E, Exton, Pennsylvania 19341.

CONNECTICUT WORKING DECOYS by Marshall Chitwood and Doug Knight.

COYKENDALL'S SPORTING COLLECTIBLES PRICE GUIDE by Ralf Coykendall, Jr. Copyright 1991. Published by Lyons and Burford Publishers.

DECOYING ST. CLAIR TO ST. LAWRENCE by Bernard W. Crandall.

DECOY COLLECTING by Ralf Coykendall. Copyright 1985, Ralf Coykendall. An edition limited to 750 soft cover copies.

DECOY COLLECTING PRIMER by Paul W. Casson. Copyright 1978 by Paul W. Casson. Out of print.

DECOY COLLECTORS GUIDE by Harold D. Sorenson. Magazine reprints from 1963 through 1977. Volumes 1-3, 1963-65 in one, hard cover volume is out-of-print. Volume 4, 1966-67, Volume 5, 1968 and Volume 6, 1977 are each still available. Plastic spiral bound.

DECOY DUCKS by Bob Ridges. Copyright 1988. Gallery Books.

THE DECOY AS ART by James A. Warner and Margaret J. White. Copyright 1985. Mid-Atlantic Press.

THE DECOY AS FOLK SCULPTURE by Swanson and Hall. Cranbrook Academy Art Museum. Copyright 1987. A catalog of a 1987 exhibit of bird and fish decoys. 1000 copies printed.

DECOYS-A NORTH AMERICAN SURVEY by Gene and Linda Kangas. Copyright 1983 by Gene and Linda Kangas. Hillcrest Publications, Inc., Spanish Fork, Utah 84660.

DECOYS AND DECOY CARVERS OF ILLINOIS by Paul W. Parmalee and Forrest D. Loomis. Copyright 1969. Northern Illinois University Press. Original edition was issued in hard cover and is out-of-print. Reissued in soft cover in 1979 and 1983.

DECOYS AT THE SHELBURNE MUSEUM by William Kehoe and David Webster. Copyright 1961, 1871. Hobby House. Out of print.

DECOYS OF MARITIME CANADA by Dale and Gary Guyette. Copyright 1983. Schiffer Publishing Ltd.

DECOYS OF THE MISSISSIPPI FLYWAY by Alan G. Haid. Copyright 1981 by Alan G. Haid. Schiffer Publishing Ltd., Box E, Exton, Pennsylvania 19341

DECOYS OF THE MID-ATLANTIC REGION by Henry A. Fleckenstein, Jr. Copyright 1979, Schiffer Publishing Ltd., Box E, Exton, Pennsylvania 19341. Hard cover edition is out-of-print with the exception of a deluxe, leather bound limited edition. Soft cover edition now available.

DECOYS: ST. CLAIR TO THE ST. LAWRENCE by Bernard Crandall. Copyright 1988. Boston Mills Press.

DECOYS OF THE SUSQUEHANNA FLATS AN THEIR MAKERS by J. Evans McKinney. Copyright 1978. Holly Press. Out of print. New revised and expanded edition, copyright 1990, published by Joe Enders, *DECOY* magazine.

DECOYS OF THE THOUSAND ISLANDS by Jim Stewart and Larry Lunman. Copyright 1991. Boston Mills Press.

DECOYS OF THE WINNEBAGO LAKES by Ronald M. Koch. Copyright 1988. Rivermoor Publications.

DOWNRIVER AND THUMB AREA MICHIGAN WATERFOWLING. THE FOLK ARTS OF NATE QUILLEN AND OTTO MISCH by Kurt Dewhurst and Marsha Macdowell. Copyright 1981. Michigan State University Press.

FACTORY DECOYS OF MASON, STEVENS, DODGE AND PETERSON by John and Shirley Delph. Copyright 1980. Schiffer Publishing Ltd., Box E, Exton, Pennsylvania 19341.

FLOATERS AND STICK UPS by George Reiger. Published by George Reiger. Copyright 1986. Out of print.

FLOATING SCULPTURE-THE DECOYS OF THE DELAWARE RIVER by Harrison Huster and Doug Knight. Copyright 1983 by Gene and Linda Kangas. Hillcrest Publications, P.O. Box 246, Spanish Forks, Utah 84660.

GEORGE BOYD, THE SHOREBIRD DECOY-AN AMERICAN FOLK ART by Winthrop L. Carter. Copyright 1978. Tenant House Press. 200 copies printed. Now out-of-print.

THE GREAT BOOK OF WILDFOWL DECOYS by Joe Engers. Copyright 1990. Abbeyville Press.

GUNNERS PARADISE, WILDFOWLING AND DECOYS ON LONG ISLAND by E. Jane Townsend. Copyright 1979. Museums at Stony Brook.

GUNNING THE CHESAPEAKE by Roy Walsh. Copyright 1961. Tidewater Publishers, P.O. Box 109, Cambridge, Maryland 21613.

JOEL BARBER'S AMERICA by Ralf Coykendall, Jr. Copyright 1983 by Ralf Coykendall. Limited Edition of 200 copies. Soft cover.

THE JUDAS BIRDS by Hugh H. Turnbull. Copyright 1983 by Hugh H. Turnbull. This is essentially a catalog of an exhibit of rare Canadian and American decoys at Musee Marsil, Museum St. Lambert, Quebec, Canada.

R.A. KNUTH-WISCONSIN/MICHIGAN DECOY CARVER, 1892-1980 by Michael Holmer. Copyright 1980 by Michael Holmer.

LAKE CHAMPLAIN DECOYS by Loy S. Harrel. Copyright 1986. Schiffer Publishing Ltd., Box E, Exton, Pennsylvania 19341.

LAST OF THE PRAIRIE CARVERS, JOHN TAX by Traff and Lindgren. Copyright 1970. Out of print.

LOUISIANA DUCK DECOYS by Charles W. Frank, Jr., Copyright 1975 by Charles W. Frank, Jr. Pelican Publishing Company.

L.T. WARD & BRO., WILDFOWL COUNTERFEITERS by Byron Cheever. No copyright date in the book. Hillcrest Publications, P.O. Box 246, Spanish Fork, Utah 84660.

THE LEM WARD STORY by Glen Lawson. Copyright 1984. Schiffer Publishing Ltd., Box E, Exton, Pennsylvania 19341.

R. MADISON MITCHELL-HIS LIFE AND DECOYS by Charles Lee Robbins. Copyright 1988 & 1989. Harve de Grace Decoy Museum. Harve de Grace, Maryland.

MARTHA'S VINEYARD DECOYS by Stanley Murphy. Copyright 1978. David R. Godine, Publisher, Boston. Out of print.

MASON DECOYS by Byron Cheever. Copyright 1974. Hillcrest Publications, P.O. Box 246, Spanish Fork, Utah 84660.

MODERN DECOYS BY JOEL BARBER. Collected and edited by Ralf Coykendall, Jr. Copyright 1985 by Ralf Coykendall, Jr.

NEW ENGLAND DECOYS by John and Shirley Delph. No copyright date listed in the book. Schiffer Publishing Ltd., Box E, Exton, Pennsylvania 19341.

NEW JERSEY DECOYS by Henry A. Fleckenstein, Jr. Copyright 1983. Schiffer Publishing Ltd., Box E, Exton, Pennsylvania 19341.

NORTHERN LAKES DECOY EXHIBIT by Jim and Mark Richards. Copyright 1982. Lake Publishing. An exhibit catalog of 11 pages. 250 copies were printed.

ONTARIO DECOYS by Bernie Gates. Book #2 published by Upper Canadian. Copyright 1982. Book #1 is out-of-print and is superseded by this latest, hard cover edition.

THE OUTLAW GUNNER by Harry M. Walsh. Copyright 1871. Tidewater Publishers, P.O. Box 109, Cambridge, Maryland 21613. This book is now in its eighth printing (1986).

PIONEER DECOY CARVERS-A BIOGRAPHY OF LEMUEL AND STEPHEN WARD by Barry, Velma and Richard Berkey. Copyright 1967. Tidewater Publishers, P.O. Box 109, Cambridge, Maryland 21613.

PORTRAIT OF A DECOY CARVER: ROBERT G. LITZENBERG by Donna Bilinko. Copyright 1990 by Donna Belinko.

SHANG: A BIOGRAPHY OF CHARLES E. WHEELER by Dixon Mac D. Merkt. Copyright 1984. Hillcrest Publications, P.O. Box 246, Spanish Fork, Utah 84660.

SHOREBIRD DECOYS by Henry A. Fleckenstein, Jr. Copyright 1980. Schiffer Publishing Ltd., Box E, Exton, Pennsylvania 19341.

SOUTHERN DECOYS OF VIRGINIA AND THE CAROLINAS by Henry A. Fleckenstein, Jr. Copyright 1983. Schiffer Publishing LTD., Box E, Exton, Pennsylvania 19341.

TRADITIONS IN WOOD (A History of Wildfowl Decoys in Canada) by Patricia Fleming and Thomas Carpenter. Copyright 1987. Camden House Publishing, Ontario, Canada.

UPPER CHESAPEAKE BAY DECOYS AND THEIR MAKERS by David and Joan Hagen. Copyright 1990. Schiffer Publishing Ltd., Box E, Exton, Pennsylvania 19341.

THE WARD BROTHERS DECOYS-A COLLECTOR'S GUIDE by Ronald J. Gard and Brian J. McGrath. Copyright 1989. Thomas B. Reel Co., 2005 Tree House, Plano, Texas 75023

WATERFOWL DECOYS OF MICHIGAN AND THE LAKE ST. CLAIR REGION by Clune Walsh, Jr. and Lowell Jackson. Copyright 1983. Gale Research.

WATERFOWL DECOYS OF SOUTHWESTERN ONTARIO AND THE MEN WHO MADE THEM by R. Paul Brisco. Copyright 1986. Boston Mills Press.

WATERFOWL HERITAGE—NORTH CAROLINA DECOYS AND GUNNING LORE by William Neal Conoley, Jr. Copyright 1983 by William Neal Conoley, Jr.

WATERFOWLING—THE UPPER CHESAPEAKE'S LEGACY by John C. Sullivan, Jr. Copyright 1987. Maplehurst Publishers. Issued in a limited edition of 1,000.

WETLAND HERITAGE—THE LOUISIANA DUCK DECOY by Charles W. Frank, Jr. Copyright 1984. Pelican Publishing Co.

WILDFOWL DECOYS by Joel D. Barber. This classic for collectors was first published by Windward House in 1934. This is a collectors edition worth much money. Subsequently Dover Publications, New York, issued it in 1954 in a soft cover edition, with several printings over the years, and is still available today although sometimes hard to locate. The Derrydale press Deluxe Edition of only fifty copies is bringing mid-level four figure prices. The is also a later (1989) Derrydale Deluxe limited edition of 2500 on the market.

WILDFOWL DECOYS OF THE PACIFIC COAST by Michael R. Miller and Frederick W. Hanson. Copyright 1991. MBF Publishing, P.O. Box 6097, Portland, Oregon 97228-6097.

WILDFOWLING IN THE MISSISSIPPI FLYWAY by Eugene V. Connett. Copyright 1949. Reissued 1984. Out of print.

WORKING DECOYS OF THE JERSEY COAST AND DELAWARE VALLEY by Kenneth L. Gosner. Copyright 1985. Art Alliance Press. Out of print.

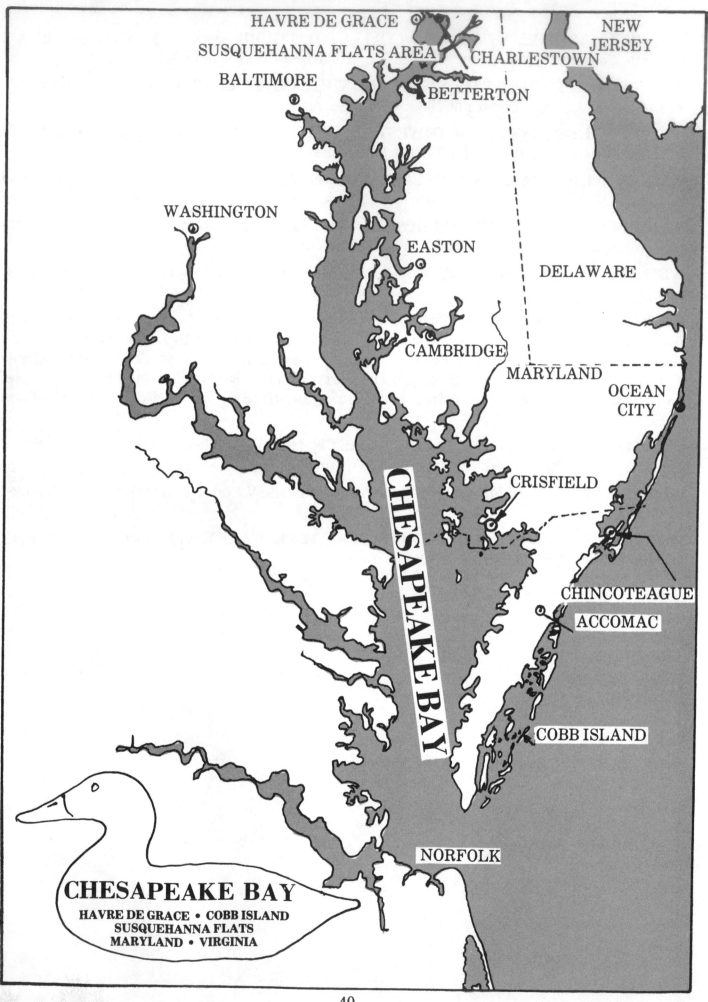

HAVRE DE GRACE

SUSQUEHANNA FLATS AREA

CHARLESTOWN

NEW JERSEY

BALTIMORE

BETTERTON

WASHINGTON

EASTON

DELAWARE

CAMBRIDGE

MARYLAND

OCEAN CITY

CHESAPEAKE BAY

CRISFIELD

CHINCOTEAGUE

ACCOMAC

COBB ISLAND

NORFOLK

CHESAPEAKE BAY

HAVRE DE GRACE • COBB ISLAND
SUSQUEHANNA FLATS
MARYLAND • VIRGINIA

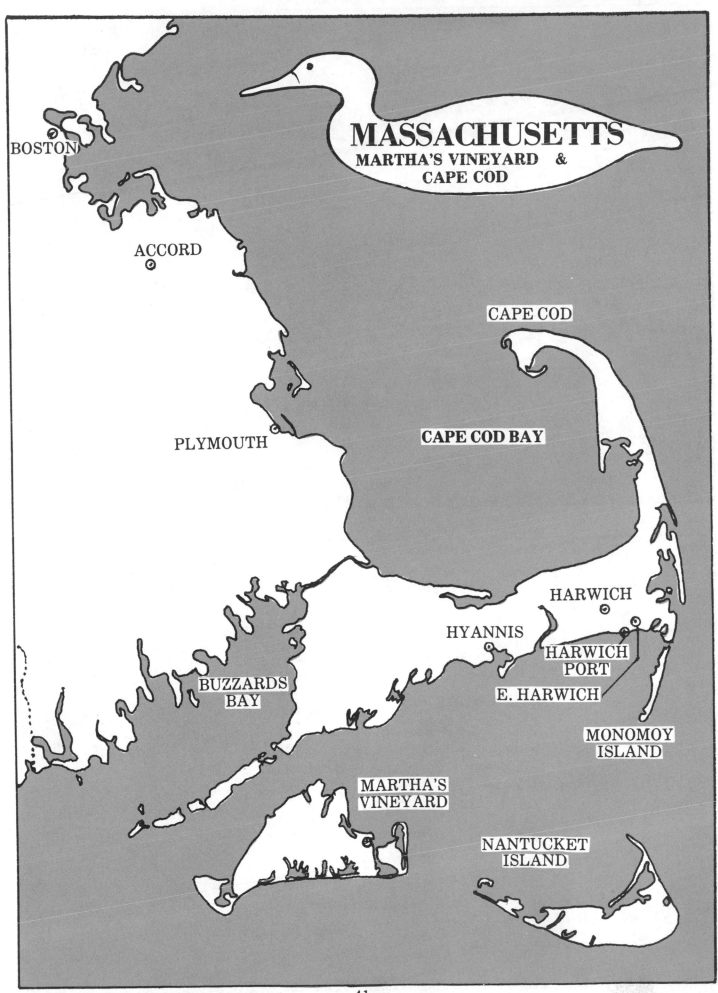

MASSACHUSETTS
MARTHA'S VINEYARD & CAPE COD

BOSTON

ACCORD

CAPE COD

PLYMOUTH

CAPE COD BAY

HARWICH

HYANNIS

HARWICH PORT

BUZZARDS BAY

E. HARWICH

MONOMOY ISLAND

MARTHA'S VINEYARD

NANTUCKET ISLAND

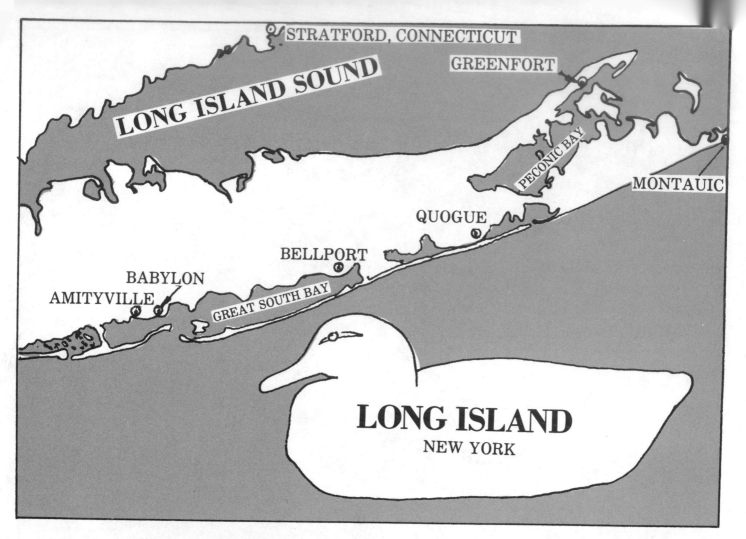

STRATFORD, CONNECTICUT

LONG ISLAND SOUND

GREENFORT

PECONIC BAY

MONTAUIC

QUOGUE

BELLPORT

BABYLON

AMITYVILLE

GREAT SOUTH BAY

LONG ISLAND
NEW YORK

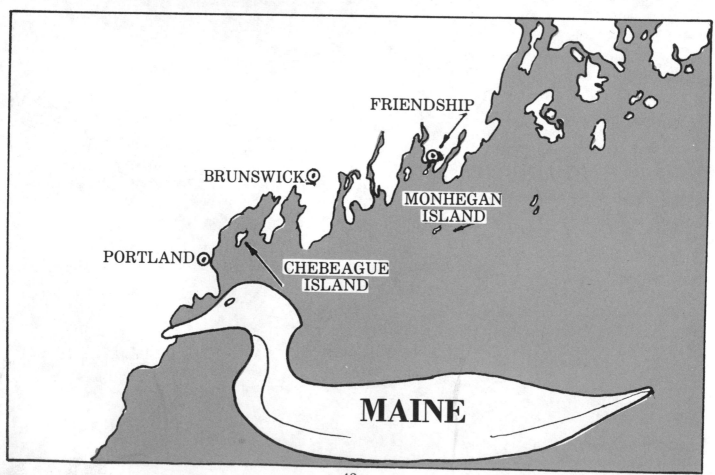

FRIENDSHIP

BRUNSWICK

MONHEGAN
ISLAND

PORTLAND

CHEBEAGUE
ISLAND

MAINE

42

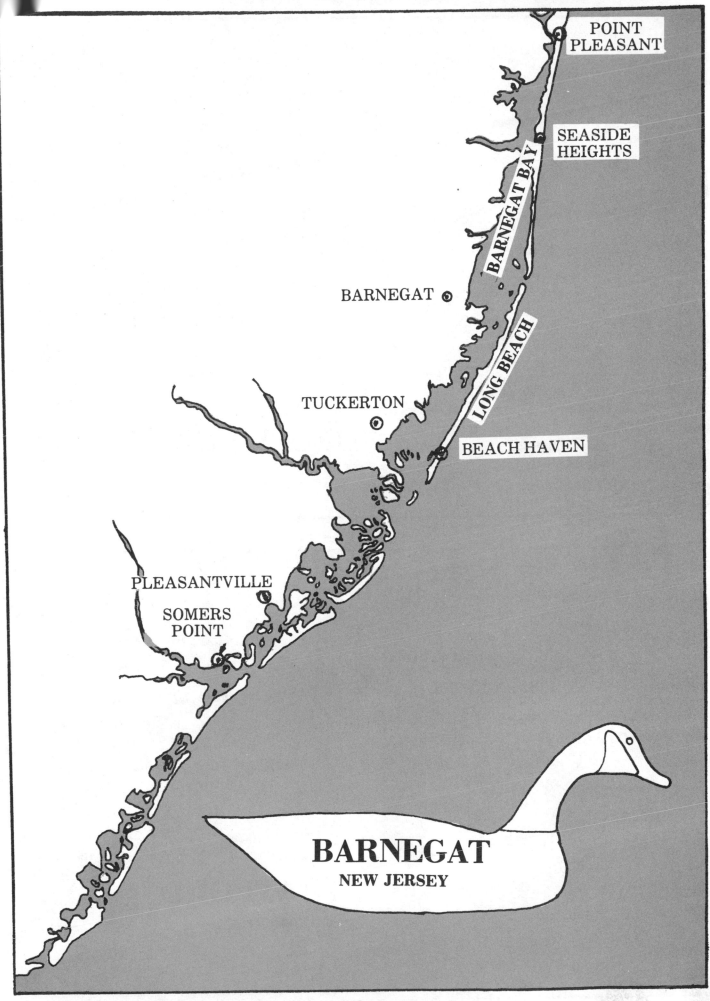

POINT
PLEASANT

SEASIDE
HEIGHTS

BARNEGAT BAY

BARNEGAT

LONG BEACH

TUCKERTON

BEACH HAVEN

PLEASANTVILLE

SOMERS
POINT

BARNEGAT

NEW JERSEY

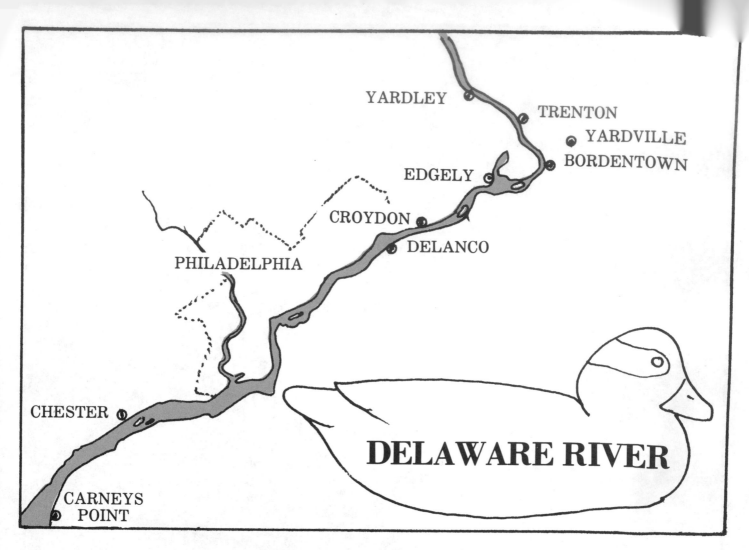

YARDLEY

TRENTON

YARDVILLE

BORDENTOWN

EDGELY

CROYDON

DELANCO

PHILADELPHIA

CHESTER

CARNEYS
POINT

DELAWARE RIVER

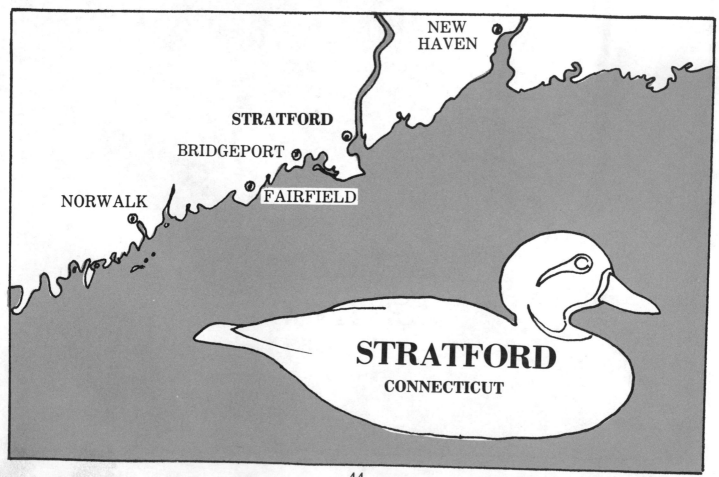

NEW
HAVEN

STRATFORD

BRIDGEPORT

FAIRFIELD

NORWALK

STRATFORD
CONNECTICUT

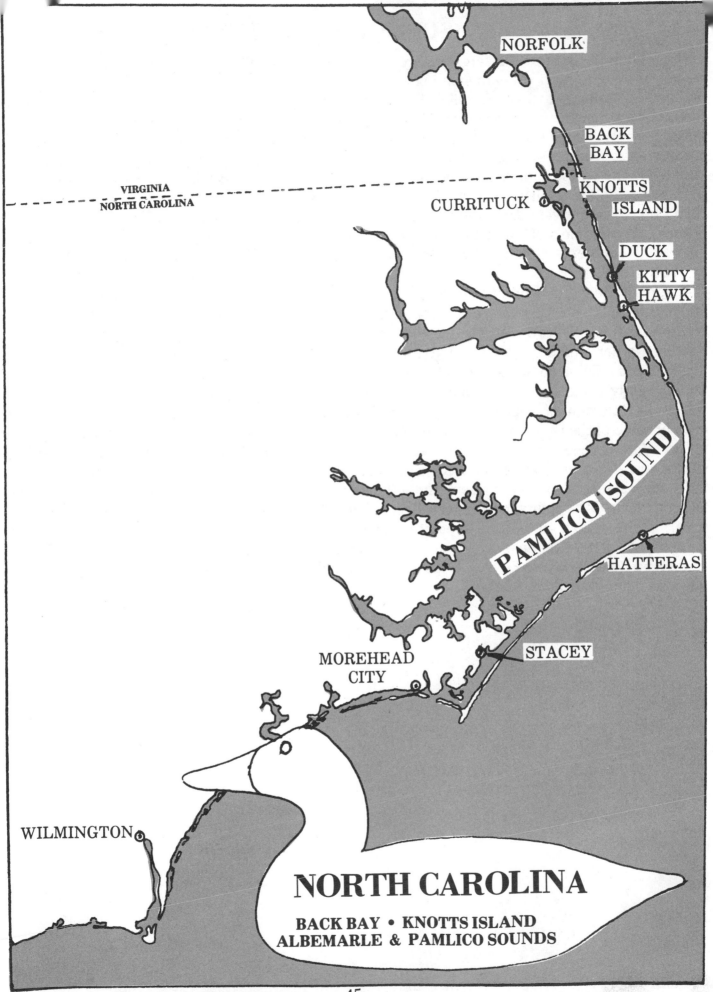

NORFOLK

BACK
BAY

VIRGINIA
NORTH CAROLINA

KNOTTS
ISLAND

CURRITUCK

DUCK

KITTY
HAWK

PAMLICO SOUND

HATTERAS

MOREHEAD
CITY

STACEY

WILMINGTON

NORTH CAROLINA

BACK BAY • KNOTTS ISLAND
ALBEMARLE & PAMLICO SOUNDS

THE SCHOOLS OF CARVERS

The schools of carvers following here are more or less regional within the various flyways. They are placed in geographical order beginning with the northernmost school in the Atlantic Flyway and proceeding southerly to South Carolina. From there we jump over to the Mississippi Flyway starting with the Louisiana School and going north all the way to Wisconsin thence over to the Pacific Flyway on the West Coast. Within each of the regional schools there are many divisions representing specific areas that are treated as separate schools by the serious collector. These smaller more specific schools are treated in detail in the various books that specialize in a study of the makers within them. To present each of these in any kind of detail would virtually require a multi-volume encyclopaedic work. The primary thrust of this book is to provide basic guidance to the new or uninformed collector. Hence, the consolidation of the smaller schools of carvers into one larger regional school in this guide. These schools are then followed by another section that discusses a few of the more important or popularly collected decoys made by "Factories."

A word of caution is in order regarding the "typical" characteristics presented in the text discussions and photo captions within each of the schools. There are few if any hard and fast rules governing these "typical" characteristics nor are there any definite line boundaries separating one school of carvers from another. Rather, each school blends into the next creating overlapping transitional areas where carvers of each were influenced by those of the other or by the changing areas and types of hunting conditions. Consequently you cannot treat a statement such as "Decoys from this school have glass eyes" as 100% true. It is a statement of what is **usually** found. There cannot be any absolutes in this regard. This is true even of some of the well-known and carefully documented makers. It is reasonable to assume that any maker might have experimented with construction or painting techniques. It is known that some of them who almost always utilized the same techniques or styles accomplished something quite different on special order for instance. Some were free with their carved heads for those carvers who could make a good body but lacked the ability to produce a decent head. There is also the case of a maker being a master at carving his decoys but lacking in painting ability and having another maker with the ability to paint them for him. The latter has occured more than once. A very good example of this is shown in Mackey's **American Bird Decoys** in PLATE 56. It shows a beautifully carved Scaup drake by Henry Keyes Chadwick that was painted by Elmer Crowell.

NOVA SCOTIA

There are at least three different sorts of decoys in the Nova Scotia school. Two are with respect to construction and the other is in paint style. The painting of most of the decoys was not very elaborate because, in the main, they hunted sea ducks not considered particularly wary. Hence the rather crude and simple paint patterns. The exception to this rule is to be found in the carving and finishing of Merganzer decoys in the south coastal area. They are generally much more sophisticated in appearance. The other two are differentiated in the manner of attaching the heads. In most of Nova Scotia carvers simply attached the head directly to the body surface. In the extreme southern area, however, they seem to have been influenced by the Maine carvers in that they utilized the inletting method of attaching the heads. A collector from Nova Scotia reports that about 80% of the decoys he has observed in the region have had inletted heads.

Bodies of typical Nova Scotia decoys are usually solid and carved from one block of pine although many are found made of two blocks. They also frequently used spruce and fir. They are characterized by flat bottoms and rounded backs for the most part. When you examine the bottom of these decoys you will often find evidence of their having been rigged "on a line," fore and aft. There may even be remnants of leather thongs present at the front and rear of the decoy bottom. Use of leather thongs was the common method of providing line ties.

Goose decoys are almost always found made of two, three or more pieces because of their size and the relative scarcity of big timber in Nova Scotia.

Value Range for Nova Scotia Decoys . . . .**$100 to $500.**

Some carvers of Nova Scotia are: Edwin Backman, Lunenberg; Orran Hiltz, Indian Point; Lindsey Levy, Villagedale and Stan Sawler from Western Shore.

PLATE 19. A drake Eider from the Nova Scotia School. The maker of this decoy is not known. Two-piece solid body with the head turned slightly to the side.

PLATE 20. A hen Eider from the Nova Scotia school. The maker of this decoy is not known. Two-piece solid body with the head turned slightly to one side.

PLATE 21. A Scoter made by Sidney Butler of Halifax, Nova Scotia.

MAINE

The drake Red Breasted Merganser shown in PLATE 22 is about as representative of a decoy from the Maine School as you can ask for. It is somewhat oversize, constructed of solid wood with a flat bottom and has very slight, faintly visible raised wing carving. The head is inletted in a manner that is common to Maine decoys as well as is the carved oval eye representation. The overall look of Maine decoys is sleek and somewhat streamlined. Although most of the paint patterns the makers used were not quite so polished as that of the Merganser pictured in the photo they are in the same stylized type pattern for the most part.

Augustus Aaron "Gus" Wilson (1864-1950) is one of the best known of makers from the Maine School. Common to all of his birds, save products of his later years, was the unusual carving of details on the underside of the lower mandible; an area of the head that few carvers ever paid much attention to as it would never be seen by a live bird being decoyed in. Other common characteristics of Wilson's decoys are the carved oval eyes, raised wing carving and carved details on both upper and lower mandibles.

Although Wilson wasn't the only one to carve decoys whose heads were ingeniously fashioned so that they would rock back and forth with wave action, if you were to find one of his rocking head Black Ducks you would have a real prize. From time to time he also carved decoys with mussels or fish in their bills, or with slots for insertion of a piece of leather or some such, simulating seaweed or fish.

Decoys from this school were generally made heavy and oversized to better fit the hunting conditions of the region. See map on page 42.

Some other Maine carvers are: Oscar Bibber, South Harpswell; George Boyd, Seabrook, NH; George Huey, Friendship; Willie Ross, Chebeague Island; Amos Wallace, West Point and James Whitney, Falmouth.

Value Range for Maine Decoys

George Huey $500-2500
*Gus Wilson
    Mergansers and Black Ducks $1000-5000
    Most others $700-3500
Other Makers from Maine $250-750

*Exceptional examples of Wilson's decoys have fetched far in excess of $10,000 at auctions.

PLATE 22. A Red Breasted Merganser drake from the Maine School. The carving and construction details of this decoy are typical of the Maine decoys and are strikingly similar to that of Gus Wilson's products. It may be one of his, but it is not substantiated.

PLATE 23. This male King Eider is placed in the Maine School because of its inletted head. As you can see it looks very much like a decoy from the Nova Scotia School. It could very well be from a transitional area between the schools but for the purposes of this book it is in the Maine School. Many collectors lump the two schools together.

MASSACHUSETTS

The Massachusetts School is where the first evidence of a widespread movement toward more refined decoys in that they are made in overall shape much more like a live bird. As a general rule however, they lack fine detailing such as wing carving or very intricate paint patterns, but they were well finished with fine sanding and the paint patterns more accurately reflect that of live birds than most earlier decoys.

An extraordinary exception to the above are the decoys of a maker from the Cape Cod area. Elmer Crowell (1862-1951) of East Harwich, Massachusetts is acknowledged to be a master among makers from any school. The decoys he made from about 1900 to 1920 are those most sought by collectors. After that period his production of working decoys began to decline while his interest in the **art** of the decoy increased and he concentrated more and more on producing decorative or ornamental decoys. Crowell used a distinctive oval brand, but he did not initiate its use until about 1915. Some collectors consider his 1900-1915 unbranded decoys as being the most desirable. The brand is illustrated below in line drawing. It measures $3\frac{1}{8}'' \times 1\frac{7}{8}''$.

Later on, (c.1930) Crowell adopted a smaller rectangular shaped brand. This later brand was also used by his son Cleon.

Elmer Crowell's decoys were made with solid white cedar bodies with heads carved from white pine as were all the typical Massachusetts School decoys. He was both an exceptional carver and painter. A common characteristic of his decoy is carved wings with the tips crossed. Additionally he used a rasp to simulate feathers on the breasts and the back of the heads. Almost all of his birds had glass eyes and the bottoms were wide and flat.

There are some decoys by Crowell that are a typical in style although his painting talent is obvious. These are from a rig he carved for the Monomoy Branting Club. They differ in construction in that they are so narrow-bodied and high that they had to be mounted on a triangular frame, usually in groups of three, to make them float upright.

As Crowell progressed his working decoys became less and less detailed insofar as carving details are concerned but, with one exception, his painting pattern remained as good as ever. This is illustrated by the fact that even when his birds lacked any wing carving at all, he still painted the wings beautifully and detailed to the point of his characteristic crossed wing tips. The exception is a group of Black Ducks he made for a sporting goods store. They are very plain with no carving detail on the body at all. The heads are characteristically rasped and the wing tips painted crossed. These decoys were stenciled on the bottom with the name of the store; "Iver Johnson."

In the photos accompanying this text is a Brant by Joe Lincoln (1859-1938) from Accord, Massachusetts. This typical Lincoln decoy was made sometime before 1920. It has a carved separation between the bill and face, glass eyes and one-piece solid cedar body.

The Canada Goose in the photo is also a Joe Lincoln decoy. The way this decoy is constructed is also common to Canada decoys of the school. The Slat-body is formed by bending lath-like narrow cedar slats over a frame. The earlier examples had canvas or similar material stretched over the body and then the finished product was painted. Later they dispenced with the practice of covering the wood with fabric and merely painted directly on the wood. The heads were carved from cedar normally. He also made very nice hollow body Canada Goose decoys that were hollowed out from the bottom, mounted on a bottom board and open at the rear, making them self-bailing.

The last carver illustrated as representative of this school is Henry Keyes Chadwick (1865-1958) of Martha's Vineyard. It is estimated that he carved upwards of 2000 decoys during his decoy making years. His birds were also the typical one-piece solid cedar bodies with pine heads. They were flat-bottomed, beautifully carved decoys usually sporting glass eyes although he sometimes used both tack and painted eye representation. Usually there will be a hole evident on the bottom, beneath the head, through which he inserted a brass screw to hold it in position. His ballast weight was flush with the bottom or inletted. He would carve out a rounded hole in the bottom and pour in molten lead to accomplish this.

Earlier decoys (pre-1920) made by Chadwick have much more slender necks, paint and carved detailed heads with metal or painted eyes and longer undercut tails than do his later ones; they could be characterized as much more delicately rendered than the later more rugged, thicker necked blocks. One interesting thing is that the later ones will more than likely sport glass eyes in countersunk sockets. Although Chadwick's paint patterns are fairly good, it is generally accepted that he was a much better carver than painter. As a matter of fact, it is known that sometimes when Crowell ran short of decoys to sell he would purchase stock from Chadwick to paint and sell.

Benjamin D. Smith (1866-1946) was a contemporary of Crowell and Chadwick and a neighbor of the latter on Martha's Vineyard. Chadwick emulated both Crowell and Smith, but Smith had the greatest influence on his work. This was so much so that sometimes it can be difficult for the less knowledgeable to tell their pre-1900 decoys apart. Subsequent to that all of Chadwick's decoys were flat bottomed, solid bodied with his distinctive flush, circular bottom lead weight. Ben Smith's decoys would sometimes be fashioned with a hollow body and rounded bottoms.

A few other carvers from Massachusetts are: Bert Hunt, Duxbury; T. Lindberg, Cape Cod; Arthur B. Rich, Duxbury; William Swift, Sagamore Beach; Charles Thomas, Assinippi and Franklin Wright, Cape Cod.

Value Range for Massachusetts Decoys

Joe Lincoln	$1000-6000*
Elmer Crowell	$600-6000**
Henry Keyes Chadwick	$300-3000***
Benjamin Smith	$500-2000

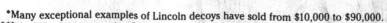

*Many exceptional examples of Lincoln decoys have sold from $10,000 to $90,000.
**It is difficult to catagorize Crowell decoys into a value range as auction sales vary accross the spectrum from mid to high four figure amounts up to mid five figure amounts with a few even going into six figures.
***Exceptional examples of Chadwick decoys have gone over $10,000.

PLATE 24. A Brant made by Joe Lincoln. Lincoln was a commerical decoy maker from Accord, Massachusetts. This Brant is beautifully formed and is a very typical Lincoln decoy with the one-piece solid body, glass eyes and a carved delineation between the bill and face.

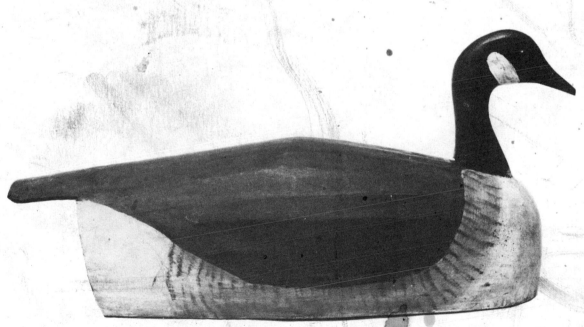

PLATE 25. Another decoy by Joe Lincoln. This is a slat-body Canada Goose. This particular decoy has a canvas cover indicating that it may be one of the earlier Massachusetts slat-body goose decoys (see text accompanying).

PLATE 26. Hen Goldeneye made by Henry Keyes Chadwick of Martha's Vineyard, Massachusetts. He made very strong and serviceable decoys that are quite typical of decoys of Martha's Vineyard makers. The flattened, turned down tail is characteristic. This decoy was made around 1925.

PLATE 27. This Chadwick Goldeneye drake is the mate to the Hen Goldeneye in PLATE 26.

PLATE 28. This is one piece of a "double shadow" decoy attributed to Joe Lincoln. The "double shadow" usually consists of eight silhouettes of ducks, six of which nest between fixed decoys at either end. Sea Coots or Scoters.

CONNECTICUT (STRATFORD)

The Stratford area was home for three masters of decoy making: Albert Laing (1811-1886), Benjamin Holmes (1843-1912) and Charles E. "Shang" Wheeler (1872-1949). These three represent the best of the makers in the area and their work is very representative of the typical styles and construction type normally used there. That these three men are the best of the school is a bit unusual in that note of them was a commerical maker. It is known that Shang Wheeler never sold any of his decoys and if either of the others did so it was probably a rare occurence. They made their decoys for themselves and friends and it is not very likely that any one of them carved more than a few hundred in their lifetime. This fairly low production probably accounts for the superb workmanship exhibited in their respective decoys.

Common to all three of them is the exaggerated upswept breasts carved to enable the decoys to float in and over ice and slush frequently encountered in the waters of the area. In addition each of them utilized a two-piece hollow body with a depression carved in the body top just behind the head. The latter is sometimes referred to as a "neck notch" or "V groove."

Even with these common characteristics they are fairly easily distinguished from each other.

When Laing carved his birds he almost invariably carved his last name quite clearly in large letters on the bottom. Even if this brand is not present you can tell his from Holmes birds because Laing always made his two-piece bodies in more or less equal upper and lower halves with the joint being above the waterline. Holmes used a half inch bottom board to close up the bottom of the hollowed out body. The best way to distinguish Wheeler decoys from the others is by being familiar with his highly sophisticated painting style. It is thought the Wheeler only produced about 500 altogether.

The majority of decoys from the Stratford area are hollow constructed with glasss eyes, the exaggerated breasts, and beautiful paint jobs often using the comb-feather technique. When bottom boards were used they will generally be of a 1/2" to 5/8" thickness. When the original weight is present it will usually be what is referred to as the Connecticut "Pear-shaped Weight." This weight, really more like a teardrop cut in half, was attached with a brass screw so that the hunter could loosen the screw allowing him to adjust the weight for balancing the floating decoy. The species most often found is the Black Duck as it was the species hunted most often.

The Pintail in the accompanying photos was made by Shang Wheeler about 1925. This decoy has its original paint and is a superb example of Wheeler's talent as a maker. Also you will find another photo of the same decoy. You will note in that photo that Wheeler took the extra trouble to apply his painting talent even to the bottom of the decoy. This is common to all of his decoys of puddle duck species.

The example of Ben Holmes decoys illustrated in the accompanying photos is like most decoys of the school that were made with bottom boards.

The Bliss Black Duck illustrated in bottom view presents the overall pear shape characteristic of decoys of the area.

As a general rule decoys of the school are of the two-piece hollow body variety. Early makers used glass eyes later evolving to painted eyes. They did not often use tack eyes apparently. See map on page 44.

Value Range for some Stratford Decoys

Ben Holmes	$500-2000
Charles "Shang" Wheeler	$1000-7000*
Roswell Bliss	$500-1200**
Albert Laing	$1000-5000

*Many exceptional Wheeler decoys have gone in far excess of this range.
**Many exceptional Bliss decoys have gone in excess of $5000.

PLATE 29. A Pintail by Charles ("Shang") Wheeler made about 1932. This excellent decoy has its original paint in quite good condition, glass eyes, detail carving of manibles, nares and differential carving between the face and bill. The body is comb-feather painted and the tail is fashioned from a piece or sheet copper.

PLATE 30. Bottom view of the same Wheeler Pintail shown above. Note the unusual comb-feather detail painting on the bottom. Few makers of any school took the extra trouble to paint the bottom of their decoys with any design at all. This is a characteristic found on all of Wheeler's puddle duck species. The ballast weight is the classic Connecticut (Stratford) adjustable pear shaped or "Teardrop" weight.

PLATE 31. A Scaup drake made by Benjamin Holmes. This decoy has glass eyes, comb-feather painting, the very typical paddle-like tail and the protruding upswept breast of the Stratford decoys.

PLATE 32. This Black Duck by Roswell Bliss serves to illustrate more common characteristics of the Stratford School; paddle tail, protruding breast and the groove behind the head.

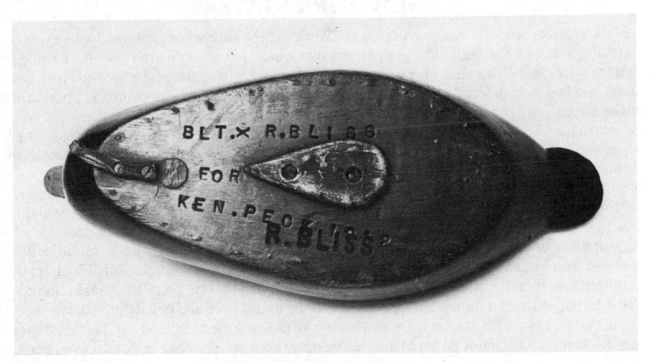

PLATE 33. Bottom view of the Bliss Black Duck in PLATE 32. Bliss used the bottom-board construction technique. Note the brand stating that the decoy was built by Bliss for Ken Peck in 1912. The Bliss brand is found on most of his pre-1940 decoys. You can also see the head-holding dowell on the bottom just aft of the anchor line tie.

NEW YORK STATE

The New York State School is more accurately the Western New York school. Although there was certainly decoy making going on through out the state, the two areas of most note are the western side of Long Island. More specifically, the area of the western side around where the St. Lawrence river flows in to Lake Ontario called Alexandria Bay and St. Lawrence Islands more commonly known as Thousand Islands and up the river to around Ogdensburg and down the western coast toward Buffalo.

The western New York School boasted very few commerical carvers, but two who did make their living as decoy makers were Frank Lewis (born c. 1880, d.?) of Ogdensburg and Samuel J. Denny (1874-1953). Their birds are good examples of decoys from this school.

Generally speaking, the typical characteristics of decoys from this school are flat bottomed, solid bodies with gently low curved backs ending in a long tail that is sometimes found pointed. Almost all are found with glass eyes. Decoys from the area of Alexandria Bay almost always have a carved horizontal "V" groove in the side of the head where the eyes are placed. The Sam Denny Goldeneye in Plate 38 shows this nicely.

Up the river from Alexandria Bay in Ogdensburg, Frank Lewis carved commercially for about ten years and his output was literally in the thousands. In fact it is known that he himself stated in one particular year alone, he carved over a thousand. He started carving about 1906 and began his commerical venture in 1920. He carved Broadbills, Redheads and Whistlers all utilizing the same body and head differentiating between the species with paint patterns and colors only. They sport rather deeply carved concave eye grooves. The heads are inletted into the body. The body itself exhibits a pronounced hump on the back. This unique characteristic gave rise to a descriptive term used by collectors: "Ogdensburg Humpbacks." See Plate 34.

Alexandria Bay carver Sam Denny made decoys commerically for over fifty years and during that period probably produced well over six thousand. One characteristic of his product you can almost always count on to help in identification is the presence of a half-inch hole (pre-1918) or two half-inch holes (1918-on) in his flat-bottomed, solid body decoys, filled with dowels rather than putty. His blocks typically have exaggerated, protruding breasts similar to those of the Stratford, Connecticut School. They do differ somewhat, in that the Denny birds have a sharp chine. The front of the breast is flattened considerably, and almost pointed at the top. He did not use inletted heads, but rather attached them to a carved shelf or raised neck seat. All his heads have a horizontal eye groove.

Value Ranges for New York State Decoys

Sam Denny	$250-1000
Frank Coombs	$300-1000
Frank Lewis	$50-250
Chauncy Wheeler	$500-3000*

*A few have sold far above this range.

PLATE 34. Frank Lewis of Ogdensburg, New York made this hen Scaup. Note the carved concave head sides. This is typical of his decoys. The bird is simply but effectively carved and painted. It has an inletted head/neck.

PLATE 35. An exceptionally graceful Sam Denny Black Duck from St. Lawrence River/Alexandria Bay area of New York State. Note the definite shelf carved to receive the head and the flattened protruding breast. The head is attached from the bottom through a recessed hole that is plugged with a cork to protect it. All characteristics typical of Denny decoys.

PLATE 36. Another New York School bird. Frank Coombs of the Alexandria Bay area made this hen Bluebill. It has a solid body, glass eyes and original paint. Ca. 1925.

PLATE 38. Another decoy made by Sam Denny. This Goldeneye drake exhibits the same characteristics as the Black Duck in Plate 35. It is a better example of the typical straight-line flattened breast on his decoys.

LONG ISLAND

The greatest number of decoys from the Long Island School are constructed of solid wood but there are a few hollow body decoys to be found. The latter will generally be flat-bottomed and somewhat undersized. This school is where root heads and cork body birds first gained widespread popularity among makers of the Atlantic Coast. The root heads are most often found on Mergansers, Pheasants, Brants and Black Ducks. The cork body decoys are usually found made in two or more layers atop a pine bottom board.

Some general observations about wooden Long Island birds are that they are usually of solid construction with a carved shelf for the mounting of the head and there is no detail carving on the face or bill. Carved eye representation, however, is very common. They sometimes used track eyes. It should also be mentioned that Long Island carvers sometimes use holly roots and pine knots for heads. These are more typically found on Sheldrake, Brant and some goose decoys. The decoys are simply constructed with no wing or feather carving. They are well sanded and simply but nicely finished in paint patterns. Often they were not painted at all, but simply given an even finish by exposing them to fire. Sadly for the collector they also were often left to lie in pines on the beach between uses.

A common ballast weight for Long Island decoys is a lead weight that has been cast in sand or the hollow in a tree limb or piece of driftwood.

The two Brants and the Black Duck in the accompanying illustrations are fairly typical of decoys from this school.

Heron, Wood Duck and Old Squaw decoys from the Long Island school are particularly rare in that order of precedence. They range in value from $750 to as high as $3000. Good Mergansers can be valued up to about $500 and other species of decoys from the school range upwards from around $75 with most topping out at about $200. See map on page 42.

Some Long Island carvers and their value ranges:

Thomas Gelston (1851-1924) $250-1000*
Frank Kellum (1865-1935) $300-1500
Obediah Verity (c1850-c1940) $1500-6000**
Al Ketchum $1000-1500**

*This range is for his duck decoys. He is more noted for his shore birds of which have fetched auction prices well into five figures.
**Shorebirds

PLATE 39. This early 20th Century Black Duck decoy was made by a well known market hunting family from Long Island. Typically they refined their decoys to the degree shown in the photo. The head is not made from a root but rather nicely carved from a block of wood and attached to the typical shelf carving through this shelf is only slightly discernable. The body is of solid wood with a flat bottom and a back groove common to Verity family decoys. The eyes are carved and their bills and faces lack any carving details. It is known that the family did do a bit of wing carving from time to time.

PLATE 40. This is another Long Island School Brant. As in the case of the other Brant the carver of this one is not known. What is known is that it came from Bellport and is about 100 years old. It has the typical shelf carving and a holly root head with brass tack eyes.

PLATE 41. A very fine Long Island Brant decoy with original paint. The maker of this decoy is not known but was obviously talented. This bird sports the typical root head found on Long Island Brant and Goose decoys but only a slight hint of the shelf for the neck/head attachment can be detected. It has carved eye representation but no face or bill carving details. Possibly carved by Lemuel and William Ackerly for W.L. Suydam (See Plate 42).

PLATE 42. This photo shows the bottom of the Brant in PLATE 41. The brand "Suydam" is quite significant in that it belonged to a very prominant Long Island family. They apparently were choosey about the decoy they hunted over for their brand shows up on many excellent decoys from the region. Another significant feature on the bottom is the presence of holes in a pattern that indicates that the decoy was used as a wing decoy. A wooden wing decoy is a rare bird indeed.

BARNEGAT BAY (NEW JERSEY)

Just about all the makers of the Barnegat Bay area in New Jersey fashioned their decoys from white cedar using the two-piece hollow body method. The heads were carved from white cedar as well. It is exceedingly unusual to find a solid body decoy from this school. Makers from the Barnegat School were masters of the two-piece hollow body style. The bodies they made are proportionally smaller than those from most of the other schools on the Atlantic Coast and the heads were slightly out of scale, being somewhat large for the bodies. The heads were attached to the body on a carved shelf. The two pieces hollowed out to make the body were joined at a seam above the waterline. The decoys were very light and for ballast the makers used pads cut from sheet lead. Most of the time these lead pad weights were attached to the bottom only after the decoy had been printed. Not all makers adhered to this practice and one notable exception was a maker named Harry V. Shourds. Shourds ballasted his decoys by carving out a rectangular hole in the bottom and pouring molten lead into it (see PLATE 46). He painted the decoy **after** this operation. Perhaps the most famous of the Barnegat Bay carvers, he is known to have been the sole contributor to his blocks from the careful selection of the wood, white pine for bodies and juniper for heads, to the final sale. His price was $6.00 per dozen. Imagine, 50 cents each! Nowadays it is not particularly unusual to see some of them sell in the low to mid four figure range.

Value Ranges for Barnegat Decoys

Harry V. Shourds (1871-1920)	$500-2000*
Ellis Parker (d.c 1940)	$200-500
Jesse Birdsall (c1852-1929)	$200-500
Charles Birdsall	$200-1000
Taylor Johnson (1863-1929)	$200-400
Walter Bush	$300-1500
Nathan Rowley Horner (1882-1942)	$1000-6000

*Average. Many sell for less and some for much more.

PLATE 43. A Brant made by Ellis Parker of Beach Haven in New Jersey. This is a classic example of white cedar two-piece hollow-body New Jersey Decoy. The joint of the two halves is above the waterline, has a leather thong for anchor line attachment. If you look closely, you may be able to discern the woodscrew eye. This is not usual. Parker apparently ran out of glass eyes and used the screws to save time. It is interesting to note the screw slots are oriented horizontally as if the bird were sleeping. Parker decoys will generally be found with ballast weight attached prior to painting.

PLATE 44. This Barnegat School Black Duck decoy was made by Jesse Birdsall. Note the definite shelf carving. It has the typical lead pad weight. You may not be able to see it but there is a faint hint of tail carving detail on this particular decoy.

PLATE 45. Black Duck by Harry V. Shourds of Tuckerton, New Jersey. This is another classic example of a New Jersey decoy with shelf, carved bill and fine details, tack eyes, and the tail extending more or less from the center of the body. This latter is characteristic of most New Jersey decoys excepting Brants and Geese. This particular decoy was found with a thick coat of a brushed on garish color that was removed.

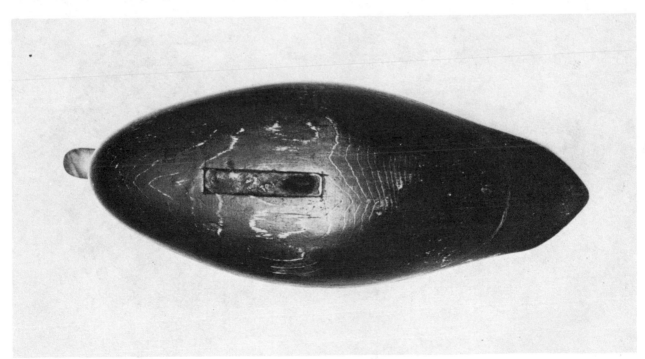

PLATE 46. This photo is of the bottom of the above Shourds Black Duck. It shows the exterior view of the inletted lead weight discussed in the accompanying text. If you were to take an X-ray of the bird, you could see that Shourds carved down and then horizontally a bit so that when the lead was poured in it turned about 90 degrees. This held the weight in the body very effectively, if it were to become loose as a result of the wood expanding or contracting.

69

PLATE 47. Widgeon Drake by Lloyd Johnson. This New Jersey decoy has pronounced flat bottom, glass eyes and excellent original paint. It has a lead pad weight that was placed on the decoy after the paint job was applied. This decoy was probably made to be used in non-coastal waters.

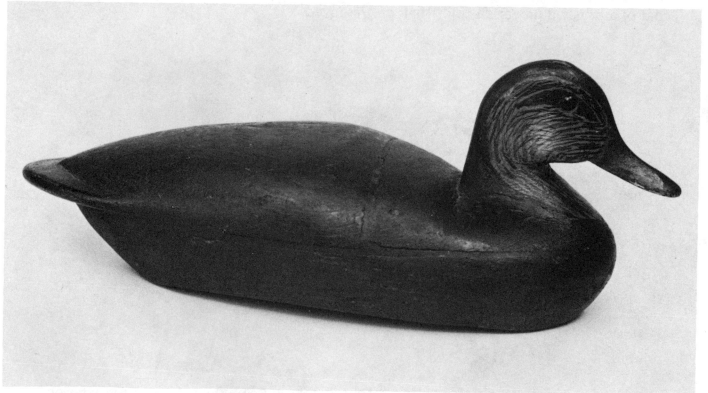

PLATE 48. Black Duck made by Walter Bush of Newark, New Jersey. Notice the unusual construction of this hollow body decoy. The upper one-half is made in two sections, the forward section being part of the head and neck.

Shelburne Museum

PLATE 202. An almost perfect condition Red Breasted Merganser made by Nathan Rowley Horner of West Creek, New Jersey. c. 1930.

PLATE 49. This New Jersey School Merganser was made by Chip Alsop. It has a two-piece hollow body, tack eyes, a neck notch and a rectangular inletted ballast weight.

PLATE 50. A Scaup drake decoy by New Jersey School maker Dipper Ortley. Ortley, from Point Pleasant, N. J., used painted eyes and the two-piece hollow body construction typical of this school. This is a fairly late decoy, having been made in the 1950's.

PLATE 51. This swimming Mallard drake is attributed to J. Eugene Hendrickson. This New Jersey maker's decoy are made in the traditional fine hollow-body New Jersey style. His tails usually end in something of a point, as is the one in the photograph here. Glass eyes and detailed bill, face carving and, often, comb feather painting characterize his birds. He frequently branded his birds with his initials "JEH."

72

DELAWARE RIVER

Decoys of the Delaware River School have hardly any rivals in other schools as a group when it comes to the beauty of carving and painting. As a whole the decoys made by the carvers of this school are considered by many, many collectors to be the most desirable from most aspects of collecting.

The method of hunting practiced in the area dictated that the decoys hunted over be made as much like the real thing as was possible. The typical hunter in the area used a sculling boat to almost bushwack the ducks. The hunter would set out his rig of decoys at known or likely feeding grounds, pull back upstream as much as three quarters of a mile and wait for the ducks to pitch in and land. He then would very carefully and silently scull down to within killing range and fire away. Because of this method the Delaware River decoy not only had to be good enough to decoy the birds down, but to still fool them once they had landed among them. The latter requirement was to give the waiting hunter time to scull back down to his prey.

The decoys had to be extremely realistic in both carving confirmation and paint pattern. Most of them have heads squat down on the body with little or no neck showing at all. This conveyed an attitude of content ducks who sense no danger, to the live ones above.

The decoys are full breasted and constructed in the two-piece hollow manner; few bottom board types were made. Heads are mounted directly to the body in the low head or sleeping position. They usually had glass eyes although the other types have been found. A very significant characteristic common to them is extremely well-carved tails and wings.

As a rule the paint patterns were extraordinarily realistic and often quite intricate.

As you go down stream on the river you find that the makers paid less and less attention to the carving of wings and tails, but they did continue to pay close attention to the need for painting their decoys in the same realistic and characteristic pattern style.

The John Dawson and John English decoys pictured in the accompanying plates serve well to illustrate the style which is that of Delaware River School of carvers.

John Dawson decoys are a bit different from his contemporaries in his paint patterns. An accomplished landscape artist, well-known in his time, he apparently applied his knowledge of paint manipulation to his decoys. He would generally block out the main areas of color pattern and then go back and very meticulously rendered feathers and other characters with hundreds of tiny brush strokes.

Value Ranges for Delaware River Decoys

John Dawson (1889-1959) $500-3000*
Dan English (1883-1962) $500-4000
John McLaughlin (b 1911) $500-2500

Some other makers of the Delaware River school are William Quinn (1915-1969) of Yardley, PA, Charles Allen (b. 1893) of Bordentown, NJ, George D. Runyan, also of Bordentown, John Baker (b. 1916) of Edgely, PA and Jess Heisler (1891-1943) of Burlington, NJ.

*There have been a few sales far in excess of this.

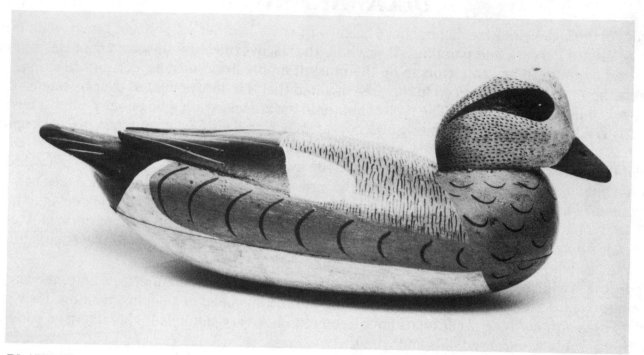

PLATE 52. A Widgeon drake made by John Dawson of Trenton and Duck Island in New Jersey. This decoy exhibits the classic squat position of the head so common to the Delaware School as well as the typical delicately sculpted wings and tail.

PLATE 53. Dan English, Florence, New Jersey, made this Black Duck. This bird shows just a hint of neck, but still the overall appearance conveys the necessary restful, contentment. The photograph doesn't do justice to the subtle beauty of the paint pattern.

PLATE 54. This Canada Goose decoy was made by M.L. Perkins of Delano, New Jersey. Delano is on the Delaware River and Perkins is part of the Delaware River School of makers. This Canada Goose has glass eyes, raised wing carving, and the body is of three-piece hollow

PLATE 55. William Quinn of Yardley, Pennsylvania, made this superb Delaware River School Black Duck sleeper. It is a hollow body decoy with glass eyes, raised wing carving, and a carved tail typical of his birds.

PLATE 56. Drake Mallard. Delaware River low head. Two-piece hollow body; glass eyes; beautifully carved tail, wings; raised feather pattern on body; face and bill detail; lead pad weight; leather thong anchor line ties.

PLATE 57. Hen Mallard mate to the drake Mallard in PLATE 56.

PLATE 201. A Greater Scaup Drake, c 1880 (left) by Capt. Dan Showell, Absecon, New Jersey and a Goldeneye Drake, c 1910 (right) by Harry Boice of Pleasantville, NY.

SUSQUEHANNA FLATS

Of all the areas of the Chesapeake Bay, the Susquehanna Flats could be considered the one where market gunners and their sink boxes reigned supreme before the 1918 migratory bird legislation. These market hunters often used several hundred decoys in their rigs, consequently there were literally thousands of decoys made in the region. The huge numbers made, notwithstanding, are not evidenced by huge numbers surviving today, although there are still many found.

The types of decoys made in the Susquehanna Flats school share similar basic construction techniques and decoy style, and the difference between these decoys and those used in other schools of the Chesapeake can also be told by observing the species of wildfowl hunted. For example, the majority of decoys from the Susquehanna Flats are Canvasbacks, Redheads and Broadbills and farther down the Bay the primary targets were puddle ducks such as Teal and Mallards. Keep in mind the enormous size of the bay; there can be a 300 mile separation between schools of carvers on the Chesapeake.

The decoys of the Flats area are generally solid pine or cedar bodied with shelf carving for the nail-attached head. One exception to this is found on decoys by some makers from Havre de Grace. **Earliest** decoys had very good carving delineation between the face and bill, carved mandibles and necks, and forged iron keels or ballast weights. Later, when lead became more readily available, the weights were cast by pouring the molten lead into depressions in sand (sand cast) or natural or gouged out depressions in wood. Less attention was paid to detail face and bill carving, but the overall conformation remained relatively unchanged. Just about all decoys from this school have round bottoms and are broad-breasted. Many marsh duck decoys are found with a slight ridge down the back.

Anchor line ties on earlier Flats decoys are usually of the leather thong type, but after around 1900-1920 the ring and staple type came into and remained in constant use all over the Chesapeake Bay.

John "Daddy" Holly of Harve de Grace, Maryland, is one of the most famous makers associated with the Susquehanna Flats.

Holly had three sons: James T. (1855-1935), William (1845-1923) and John Jr. (1852-1927). James apparently operated independent of his father and brothers as a decoy maker. He was a craftsman who built fine boats primarily, but his decoys are also sought after. He is known most for the slim and sleek black duck decoys he fashioned, but he is known to have carved other species. He is thought to be one of the first to bring the scratch paint method to the Flats carvers. His father, John "Daddy" Holly carved and painted in several different styles over the years. He is, however, thought to have established the Harve de Grace style, upswept tails and no neck shelf on diving and marsh ducks. Upon his death in 1892, his two other sons, William and John Jr., undertook to continue the his decoy making operation. They followed their father's patterns and style and this sometimes leads to confusion among collectors. Whatever the case, any decoy made by the Hollys is desirable.

As alluded to above there are two distinct styles to be found in the Susquehanna Flats school. The first is the Harve de Grace style. The other is thought to have been founded by John B. Graham of Charlestown. Known as the Cecil County or Northeast River style these decoys feature shelf carving for the head/neck and a straight tail protruding from the middle of the rear of the body.

Ben Dye of Perryville, Maryland is one of the most respected carvers of the Cecil County style of the Flats. His heads were of exceptional quality with finely carved mandible, nails, ridges and nostrils on the bills. His decoys tended to be smallish compared to the real thing. The tails tended to be of the small flat paddle type. His earliest blocks were decidedly flattened and the later ones are found quite rounded.

Samuel T. Barnes of Harve de Grace is as well known name of the school as any. The one characteristic most easily used in beginning to identify a Barnes decoy is his curious flattening of the head from the face down the crown and onto the bill itself. His decoys otherwise exhibit the typical Flats characteristic in the Harve de Grace style. He is also known to be one of the earliest makers of cork-body decoys. They had pine heads and bottom boards.

R. Madison Mitchell began making decoys in 1924 by helping Sam Barnes in his shop. When Barnes died, Mitchell stayed on to finished unfilled orders. He apparently became more interested than just finishing up the orders for he continued making decoys for over fifty years. Although he hand fashioned them as Barnes had for five or six years, in 1931 he had begun to turn out bodies on a lath after having rough cut them from cedar blocks. He then went back to hand techniques with spokeshave, sandpaper, etc. The decoys were hand painted in high quality finishes. He added cast lead ballast weights after painting. The final touch was a staple and ring line tie.

Value Ranges for Susquehanna Flats Decoys

John "Daddy" Holly (1818-1892) $500-4000
Ben Dye (1821-1896) $150-500
R. Madison Mitchell (b. 1901) $150-500*
Sam Barnes (1847-1926) $200-600
John B. Graham (1822-1912) $200-600

*His swans will bring from $1000 to $3000.

PLATE 58. A very early Susquehanna Flats Drake Canvasback decoy made by Ben Dye of Harve de Grace, Maryland. This decoy is about as good an example of early Flats decoy as you could ask for. It has the forged iron keel driven into the bottom (sometimes called a "horseshoe keel"); a solid color rounded bottom body; eyes impressed (Dye and many other early makers used a 32 calibre shell casing to impress the eyes into the wood); and fine carving details on the face and bill.

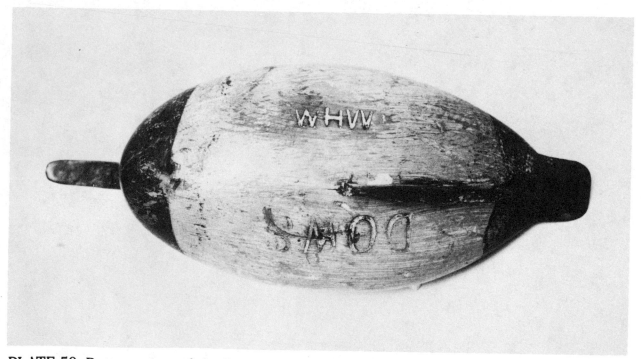

PLATE 59. Bottom view of the Ben Dye Canvasback in Plate 58. This shows user brands "WHW" and "DOWS" and the forged iron keel driven into the bottom. "DOWS" was Thomas Dows and "WHW" was his grandson, Watson Henry Webb. This type of provenance is valuable in determining vintage.

PLATE 60. A hen Canvasback made by Susquehanna Flats maker Charles Barnard. A hen Canvasback is difficult to locate generally. This is one of a pair of Barnard Canvasback (see Plate 61). It illustrates the common Flats decoy characteristics and conformation and serves well to illustrate the cast lead weight discussed in the accompanying text.

PLATE 61. The drake Canvasback, mate to the above Charles Bernard hen Canvas back. Matched pairs such as this are difficult to obtain as hens are seldom found.

PLATE 62. A very old hen Canvasback by John B. Graham of Charleston, Maryland. This is quite typical of Graham's Canvasbacks. Note the cast lead weight. This is the original weight and is one of the earliest examples of cast lead weighted decoys from the Susquehanna Flats.

PLATE 63. A bottom view of the Graham Canvasback in the preceding plate. Excellent view of his typical lead weight. The ring and staple anchor line tie common to many Susquehanna Flats decoys is evident in this photo. The "P.K. Barnes" brand is found on many good early Flats decoys.

PLATE 64. A drake Canvasback by Scott Jackson that illustrates a little different style than the ordinary Susquehanna Flats decoy. It has a long upward swept tail not common in decoys from this school nor is it characteristic of Canvasback ducks. Just about all Jackson's decoys have this slightly upswept tail.

PLATE 65. R. Madison Mitchell made this Canvasback drake from the Susquehanna Flats. He made decoys from the 1930's up to around 1960 and collectors will likely encounter one of his decoys, if seeking decoys from the Chesapeake Bay area. He was an undertaker in Harve de Grace, Maryland, and probably made more wooden decoys than any other maker in Maryland. The ring and staple anchor line tie was just about always used by Mitchell. He made all his canvasbacks just like the one in this photo.

PLATE 66. A Charlie "Speed" Joiner drake Canvasback. Joiner was from Betterton, Maryland, on the Susquehanna Flats. This decoy has ring and staple anchor line tie and typical shape cast ballast weight.

PLATE 67. This is a following two-dimensional Canvasback shadow decoy rig. Said to have come from the Chesapeake Bay area. Unsubstantiated.

PLATE 68. "Daddy" Holley drake Scaup. From Harve de Grace, Maryland, "Daddy" Holley's decoys are from the Susquehanna Flats School. Note the iron keel driven into the bottom of the decoy.

PLATE 69. A solid body, painted eye decoy from the Susquehanna Flats. Made by Paul Gibson of Harve de Grace, Maryland.

PLATE 70. Canvasback hen by R. Madison Mitchell from Harve de Grace, Maryland. Painted eyes and ballast weight typical of his decoys. From the Susquehanna Flats School.

PLATE 71. Pre-1900 Canvasback drake from Chesapeake Bay made by Henry Lockhard from Elk Neck, Maryland. Ring and staple. May have had tack or glass eyes at one time-now painted. Susquehanna Flats School.

PLATE 72. A Scoter by R. Madison Mitchell from Harve de Grace, Maryland. Painted eyes, ballast weight and ring and staple anchor line tie typical of this oversize Susquehanna Flats, Mitchell decoy.

PLATE 73. A nice Susquehanna Flats Canvasback decoy by Robert S. Sellers. This maker is still hunting in the Flats and uses the old scull boat method of hunting.

PLATE 74. A Susquehanna Flats decoy made by Walter D. Sellers. Sellers, now deceased, was the brother of Robert S. Sellers.

MARYLAND EASTERN SHORE
(DORCHESTER COUNTY)

Although this is not really considered a true school of makers, there was a commerical decoy maker of note from Cambridge, Maryland, whose birds as well worth pursuit. Ed Phillips sold most of his decoys to hometown people and for a few gunning rigs. His decoys haven't achieved the prominence of some other decoys of the Chesapeake Bay area because he didn't produce them in nearly the numbers some of the other good carvers of the region produced. They are, however, excellent decoys. The decoys are not quite so rounded bottom as others of the region but are semi-rounded (not completely rounded nor completely flat-bottomed). The bodies are quite graceful and necks usually exhibit a backward arch. Almost all have carved eye representation, very well made and painted. Phillips frequently used the scratch feather painting technique.

All Phillips decoys have a sheet lead ballast weight on the bottom and an anchor line tie made of sheet copper bent into a loop and attached with a copper nail, if the original is present.

The bodies are solid as is characteristic of Chesapeake Bay area decoys. The necks are attached by a dowel rod. He made Canvasbacks, Pintails, Widgeon, Black Ducks, Redheads, and Canada Geese. See map on page 40.

Value Ranges for Maryland Eastern Shore Decoys

Ed Phillips $700-2000

PLATE 75. An Ed Phillips drake Pintail decoy. A solid body decoy with carved eyes and scratch feather painting. This decoy illustrates the semi-round bottom discussed in the accompanying text. A beautifully carved and painted decoy by this Cambridge, Maryland, commerical decoy maker.

PLATE 76. This Canada Goose is also by Ed Phillips. If you look closely at the back of the head you can see the neck-attaching dowel rod protruding slightly. This long dowel is typical of the way Phillips attached his head/necks.

CRISFIELD (MARYLAND)

Just about all decoys from his school of carvers exhibit the same construction details. They are solid body decoys typical of the Chesapeake Bay birds, but here is where the first appearance of the true flat-bottomed decoys occurs in the bay. Typically Crisfield decoys are slightly oversize, narrow breasted, wide in the hip area, and flat-bottomed with a tail usually coming out of the top of the body as opposed to below, toward or at the middle of the rear end. The decoys were weighted with just about anything that might be handy to the maker at the time, so it is not a reliable characteristic.

The beginning of the fine decoys of the Crisfield School are thought to be found in the Sterling family and perhaps Elwood Dize products. The most famous of the school are the Ward brothers, Lemuel T. Ward, Jr. (1896-1984) and Stephen Ward (1895-1976). Their Father, Lemuel T. Ward, was a barber, but also a decoy maker, a waterman and boat builder. Lem and Steve followed in their father's footsteps also becoming barbers and decoy makers albeit the latter in their spare time, for their own use. Lem Sr. died in 1926 and not long after that came hard economic time for the nation, the depression. A greater demand was placed on the market hunters of the day as a result. Greater public demand for cheap meat made a greater demand for decoys on the part of the market hunters so the Ward brothers went ot making decoys in quantities indeed. It is estimated that they produced as many as 10,000 in the fifty years they were actively producing decoys. It was the Wards who took the carving and painting techniques of their father and the other early Crisfield makers developed and refined them to a high art. The Wards are recognized by collectors today as the most deserving of note of all the Maryland makers. The carving and painting used on their *working* decoys was as good as much of the delicate work found on todays contemporary carvings. They are painted so beautifully that people began buying them, not for hunting over, but for use as decorative objects in the home. It is known that Steve lamented the constant interruptions by those seeking their blocks, but that Lem became more and more interested in them as an art. Whatever the case, when demand for good hand-made stools waned in the 1950's the Wards went into the making of decorative decoys in earnest and didn't slow down until the early 1970's.

Other makers of note from the Crisfield school are Lloyd Tyler (1898-1971) and the Tyler family, Noah B. Sterling, Will Sterling, and Elwood Dize.

Value Ranges for Crisfield Decoys

Ward Brothers $1000-5000*
Sterling Family $300-1200

Decoys from both of these groups have brought far in excess of these figures from time to time but the ranges above are the norm for an average shape working decoy. See map on page 40.

*Some are valued at up to $8000 and occasionally will fetch low to mid five figures at auctions.

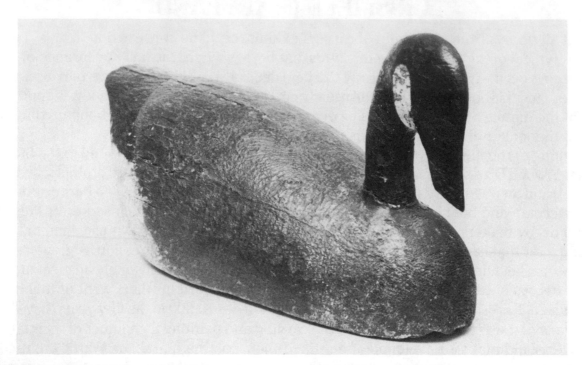

PLATE 77. This c. 1900 Canada Goose is a very early Crisfield decoy attributed to the Sterling family. Exhibits characteristics common to the school, i.e., the narrow breast, wide hips and flat bottom.

PLATE 78. Hen Goldeneye by Noah Sterling made around 1915.

PLATE 79. This Canada Goose decoy was made about 1920 by L. Travis Ward Sr. It is a fine example in original paint. Shows the beginning of the refinement in construction and paint techniques begun by the Wards. Excellent example of scratch feather pattern painting technique.

PLATE 80. A Ward Brothers balsa body Pintail drake. Keeled with the weights attached.

PLATE 81. Drake Pintail carved by Steve Ward Jr. and painted by Lem Ward. Made of balsa wood. Although this one has no eyes, that is not significant. They occur with no eyes, painted eyes and glass eyes. This particular decoy and the following mate in Plate 82 are both from the Ward Brothers' personal hunting rig.

PLATE 82. Hen Pintail by the Ward Brothers. A match to the Drake Pintail in Plate 81.

94

PLATE 83. A Ward Brothers Canvasback Drake in original paint. This decoy is solid cedar, has glass eyes and is a classic 1936 model Ward Brothers Canvasback. Collectors call these decoys "Classic '36's".

VIRGINIA EASTERN SHORE

The majority of decoys from this region are of the solid-body, round bottom type with the remaining minority being hollow. There is quite a variety of types of decoys from this school; therefore the best way to familiarize you with them is to discuss a selected group of representative makers.

Ira Hudson (1876-1949) of Chincoteague, Virginia, was the most prolific maker in the region. It is estimated that he produced over 20,000 decoys in his decoy-making days. Hudson made a number of different types, both solid and hollow-bodied. He was a commerical decoy maker and the type, style and sophistication of his products was largely dependent upon what his customers could afford. They ranged from very simply made and painted decoys to two-and three-piece hollow-bodied decoys with much detail carving, but the majority are solid-body. His choice of wood was white pine, but Hudson decoys have been found in cedar, cypress, balsa and cottonwood. Eyes were generally tack eyes or painted. He seldom utilized glass eyes. He often used the scratch feather painting technique. Carved neck notches or "thumbprint carving" are sometimes found on the back behind the neck.

In all the variations in type of decoy his painting technique and style remained constant and after handling and studying several the collector should be able to readily recognize it. The photos accompanying show a representative range of his decoy styles.

The usual method Hudson used to attach head to body was to place the neck down into a carved out hollow, although he utilized other methods such as the neck shelf carving. Hudson is also noted for using unusual head positions. Not always, but much of the time he accomplished this by carving the heads from driftwood or roots.

Dave "Umbrella" Watson (d. 1938) was a commerical maker from Chincoteague, Virginia, whose style was a blend of Eastern Shore Virginia and New Jersey construction and styles, easily distinguished from the New Jersey decoys by the presence of delicate raised wing and tail carving detail. The Watson decoy is of two-piece hollow body construction usually. A reasonable estimate of each would be 90 percent hollow and 10 percent solid body. The decoys were well sanded before painting. The painting was always well done and all his birds sport glass eyes placed in a carved eye groove. Most are carved from white cedar in two halves joined above the waterline.

Miles Hancock's (1888-1974) decoys were all solid body, constructed with flat bottoms. Most of his decoys were carved from cottonwood, a soft, easy to carve wood. He first roughed the shape out then did his finishing with pieces of broken glass. He never sanded them before painting and his painting technique was not very refined. The result of this is rough but surprisingly effective overall. He supposedly never used glass eyes, sticking to tack eyes exclusively. There have been a few to show up with glass eyes, but these may have been later replacements by the users.

Charles Birch (1867-1956) of Willis Wharf, Virginia, made decoys that were quite similar to New Jersey decoys in the general overall look of them. His decoys were the two-piece hollow body mostly with a few solid decoys that still had the appearance of being hollow-bodied. There are two significant variances from the New Jersey decoys that make them easily identifiable as Birch products. All his decoys will have a definite flat spot on the top of the body about three-fourths of the length back from the breast toward the tail. Another distinctive detail is the use of a reinforcing wooden dowel peg inserted from the bottom and visible from there.

Birch always used a shelf carving to receive the head, nailed on pad weights and his geese and swans had inletted oak or hickory bills. The latter were inserted fully through the head and tightened in the back of the head by driving a spline into a split at that end of the bill piece. See map on page 40.

Value Ranges for Eastern Shore Virginia Decoys

Ira Hudson $500-3000*
Dave "Umbrella" Watson $500-2500
Doug Jester $300-750
Charles Birch $400-1200**
Miles Hancock $200-1500

PLATE 84. Hooded Merganser drake by Ira Hudson. This decoy illustrates the "football body" and "banjo tail" often by him. Note the fluted carving on the tail, characteristic of many of his more elaborately carved birds. Tack eyes and bill carving are also present.

*A fair number exceed this, but rarely exceed five figures.
**Brants and goose decoys will frequently sell in excess of $2000. The rare swans bring extraordinary prices at auction.

PLATE 85. An Ira Hudson Black Duck. Although this decoy does not have the "banjo tail," the fluted carving can be readily seen. A very fine example of scratch-feather painting.

PLATE 86. This is a very typical Ira Hudson Scaup decoy. The high crown head and flattened breast characteristics are common to his decoys of this species. They are often found with "banjo tails." The usual local name in the Virginia Eastern Shore area for this species is "Blackhead."

PLATE 87. An exceptional Ira Hudson Canvasback drake in original paint. Note the scalloped breast feather painting and "banjo tail" often used by Hudson.

PLATE 88. This Brant by Ira Hudson has a two-piece hollow body with the joint above the waterline. Note the neck notch or "thumbprint carving" behind the neck and the carved shelf neck attachment.

PLATE 89. This hissing Canada Goose decoy made by Ira Hudson has a solid body but they are also found with hollow bodies.

PLATE 90. A Black Duck by Dave "Umbrella" Watson that is a very good illustration of the characteristics of a typical Watson decoy. Glass eyes in a carved eye groove; slight amount of delicate raised wing carving; and the above-the-waterline joint of the two-piece hollow body.

PLATE 91. A drake Blackhead made by Ira Hudson of Chincoteague, Virginia.

PLATE 92. Widgeon drake by Miles Hancock of Chincoteague, Virginia.

PLATE 93. Doug Jester Black Duck decoy. Jester is in the Virginia Eastern Shore School.

PLATE 94. Miles Hancock swimming Canada Goose. This flat-bottomed rough finished decoy is carved from native Virginia cottonwood; body, neck and head. It has tack eyes and is almost crude in painting; nevertheless it comes up rather nicely as you can readily see.

PLATE 95. Another decoy by Miles Hancock. This drake Widgeon is a very good example of how hurried the painting of his birds usually look. Notice, however, the use of scratch feather painting so common to decoys of the Virginia Eastern Shore.

PLATE 96. A Brant by Miles Hancock. Solid cottonwood with tack eyes and typical crude paint pattern.

PLATE 97. Black Duck by Charles Birch of Willis Wharf on the Eastern Shore of Virginia. It has a very prominent shelf carving to receive the neck, tack eyes and has a two-piece hollow cedar body, as do most of his birds.

PLATE 98. This drake Canvasback is another Charles Birch decoy. The above-the-waterline joint for the two halves of the hollow body can be easily seen in this photo. Exhibits typical Birch characteristics.

PLATE 99. A Canada Goose by Charles Birch. This fine decoy has a shelf carving, tack eyes, inletted hardwood bill, reinforcing wooden dowel peg and is a two-piece hollow-bodied.

PLATE 100. A solid body Black Duck made by Doug Jester. This typical Jester decoy has scratch feather painting. As so many of the good Virginia Eastern Shore makers were, Doug Jester was from Chincoteague. He always made solid body birds with shelf carving for the neck and head. The mandibles always had some carving details. This decoy has no eyes, but the horizontal line in the eye area is frequently seen on his products.

COBB ISLAND

Cobb Island, off the Eastern Shore of Virginia, is now uninhabited but was the home of the Cobb family. Nathan Cobb and his family settled on the island in 1833 as the result of a shipwreck. The family has sailed south from New England and whatever their destination originally had been, the island (subsequently named after them) became their home. They became market gunners, hunting guides, ship salvagers and of necessity, decoy carvers. The decoys they made were unlike those of other Eastern Shore Virginia makers. They apparently adhered to the methods that were common to the area of their former home. Their decoys are much like those of Massachusetts.

Many of the Cobb Island decoys are found with the initial "N" or "E" and an occasional "A" carved on the bottom. The initials are of Nathan, Jr., Elkenah and Albert or Arthur.

Generally the decoys were made slightly oversize and they are two-piece hollow body mostly but some were solid body. The ballast weights were sheet or flattened lead and always attached with brass screws. Head and neck is inletted into the hollow body. It is significant to note that inletting into **hollow** bodies is unusual. Frequently this inletted head and neck includes a portion of the breast as well. The bills on the greater proportion of the Cobb family's larger species of birds are inletted into the head. Made of hardwood they extend all the way through the head and are splined at the back of the head. You may note that Charles Birch of the Virginia Eastern Shore practiced this, but he was a later maker and probably emulated the Cobbs.

The Cobb birds are particularly noted for the many different life-like attitudes of heads; each decoy being different. This was accomplished by their extensive use of roots or driftwood to fashion the heads.

The decoys are usually flat bottomed but some are found with round bottoms.

The Cobbs established quite an active hunting lodge on the island and catered to many, many hunters during their tenure on the island. The family and some employees were involved in decoy making, but apparently Nathan Cobb, Jr. was the master. He was able to capture the very essence of a live bird with only the slightest carving gesture. His decoys were not in and of themselves perfect anatomical replicas of the birds, but possessed a spark of life seldom captures by other carvers. Each of his birds was different as noted earlier. Nathan was able to use this to an exquisite degree. He didn't so much carve individual birds as he created rigs. His individual birds, when used together, gave the impression of a flock of live birds rather than a bunch of decoys.

Split wing/tail carving is common to their birds, as is the use of glass eyes. There are, however, a goodly number with no eye representation at all.

Painting was life-like and effective but lack sophisticated detailing.

There have been some extraordinarily high prices realized at auction, but most average decoys from the Cobb family would be valued between $500 and $3000. Decoys by Nathan Cobb bring considerably more on the average. His will generally run between $4000 and $10,000, with some exceeding this considerably. See map on page 40.

PLATE 101. Black Duck made by Nathan Cobb Jr. around 1870. It has a two-piece hollow white cedar body and pine head with glass eyes. Head, neck and portion of breast is inletted. The split tail, wing carving and sheet lead ballast weight attached with brass screws completes the list of typical Cobb black duck decoys.

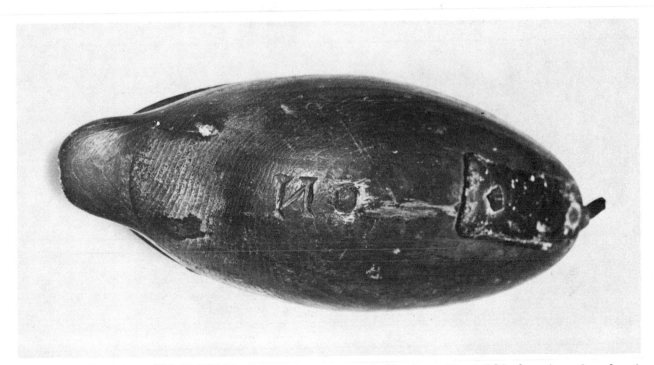

PLATE 102. Bottom view of the Nathan Cobb Black Duck in Plate 101 showing the sheet lead ballast weight and the initial brand "N" is actually carved backwards on the decoy.

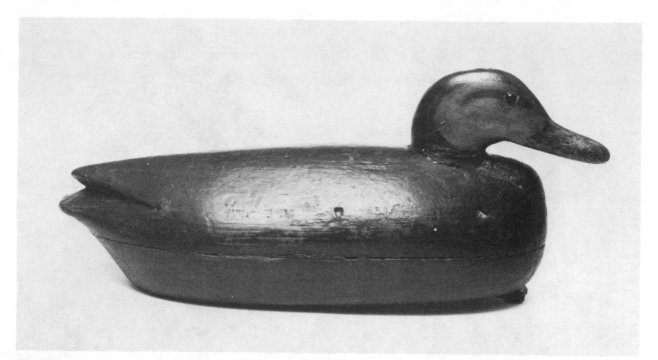

PLATE 103. This Black Duck made by Elkenah Cobb exhibits all of the typical Cobb characteristics discussed in the caption for Plate 101. Note that the carving style differs a bit. Elkenah Cobb apparently didn't carve his birds with the high rounded back typical of his father Nathan's decoys.

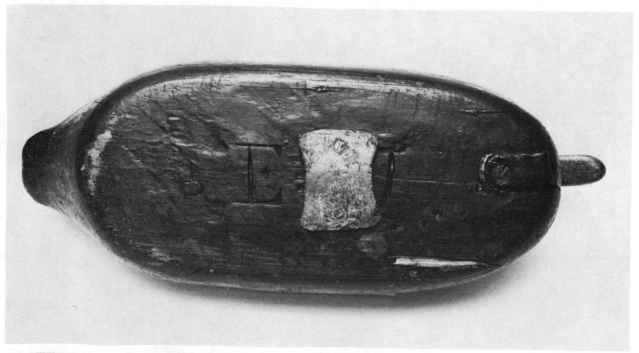

PLATE 104. A bottom view of the Elkenah Cobb Black Duck decoy showing his initial brand "E."

108

PLATE 105. This pre-Civil War Canada Goose was made by Nathan Cobb Jr. It has an inletted head/neck, typical split tail/wing carving and is two-piece hollow bodied. The head has glass eyes and an inletted hardwood bill.

PLATE 106. A close-up view of the back of the head of the Canada Goose in Plate 105 showing the peg-end of the inletted bill. If you look closely, you can see the spline that was driven into the end. This technique is discussed in more detail in the accompanying text on Cobb Island decoys.

PLATE 107. This is a **solid** body Brant decoy made by a member of the Cobb family. It has a very nice locust root head with an inletted bill. In this case, the entire face is inletted, not just the bill.

PLATE 108. Bottom view of the Brant in Plate 107. Note the hole in the bottom. This enabled the decoy to be used as a stick-up field decoy as well as a floater.

PLATE 109. A Cobb family Brant decoy in a style slightly different from the norm. It is round bottom solid body bird with the typical root head and split wing/tail. Note the hole in the side of the breast. The hole on each side was for the insertion of a brass, copper or bronze wire bent in a shape similiar to a doctor's stethoscope. Weighted at the bottom, this device imparted a bobbing motion with wave action, resulting in a very life-like simulation of a feeding Brant.

NORTH CAROLINA

This school of carvers also includes a portion of Virginia just north of the state line called Back Bay. The decoys of the Black Bay area and those of coastal North Carolina are indistinguishable for the most part.

The North Carolina School is particularly noted for its slightly oversize Ruddy Ducks. They have been called crude by many, but the overall appearance of most examples is pleasing. The most striking feature of the decoys is the very nicely shaped head on them. None are finely finished but still they are effective. Eyes are usually not present or simply painted on.

Most makers concentrated on solid body, round or semi-"V" bottom decoys. One exception are the decoys of Ned Burgess who made his birds with flat bottoms.

There were wire frame Geese and Swans made in the region. Although they do appear to be very nice decoys in the accompanying plates, they would have to be considered somewhat crude if compared to one made by Massachusetts maker Joe Lincoln.

A significant characteristic common to most North Carolina decoys is the type of anchor line tie used. If you glance at the decoys in the accompanying photographs, you will note most of them have a prominent nail protruding from the lower portion of the breast. Less obvious is the actual line tie somewhat below and behind. The purpose of the breast nail is to provide a means of lenghtening or shortening the anchor line. This was necessary because of the large tide fluctuations in the area. The hunter could choose his length by using a half-hitch to the nail and letting the extra line simply hang beneath the decoy.

A ballast weight that was often used in the Back Bay and upper North Carolina areas is shown on the decoy in Plate 113.

Some carvers of note from this school are: Lem (1861-1932) and Lee (1861-1942) Dudley, twins from Knotts Island, North Carolina; John Williams (1857-1937), Cedar Island, Virginia; Ned Burgess (1863-1956), Church's Island, Virginia; Mitchell Fulcher, Stacy, North Carolina and Alvira Wright, town of Duck, Knotts Island, North Carolina.

Value Ranges for North Carolina Decoys

Lem and Lee Dudley $2000-10,000
Ned Burgess $200-500
John Williams $3000-6000
Alvira Wright $4000-10,000*
Mitchell Fulcher $2000-10,000

*Some will go much higher.

PLATE 110. This stately looking Canvasback from North Carolina was made by Alvira Wright from Duck, North Carolina. It is a big heavy solid body bird with a rather massive ballast weight. In spite of this the bird floats only about one and one-half inches deep. Wright was also a boat builder. His decoys obviously reflect his skill and knowledge of the craft.

PLATE 111. A Ned Burgess Ruddy Duck. Burgess was from Church's Island, Virginia, and is the exception to makers of his school in that he generally produced **flat** bottom decoy. Note the prominent nail protruding from the breast. This North Carolina School characteristic is discussed in the accompanying text.

PLATE 112. This classic North Carolina Ruddy Duck is from Knott's Island. The maker is not known.

PLATE 113. A Ned Burgess Canvasback that has never been hunted over. It bears a ballast weight typically used in the upper portion of the North Carolina School. This particular weight has the initials "NPW" cast into the surface. The initials are of Nelson Price Whittaker who ran a foundry that made, among other things, ballast weights and cast iron wing decoys.

PLATE 114. A very nice Lee and Lem Dudley Ruddy Duck. The brothers were from Knott's Island, North Carolina. Note the typical protruding nail and cast weight. They always cast their own weights.

PLATE 115. This is a bottom view of the Dudley Ruddy Duck in Plate 114. It is difficult to see, but the "LD" brand the Dudleys almost always used on their decoys is above the ballast weight.

PLATE 116. An extremely nice wire framed canvas-covered Swan decoy. The maker is not known but it is from the Currituck Island, North Carolina, area.

PLATE 117. A wire frame, canvas covered Canada Goose made by Ned Burgess. North Carolina is one of the very few places where the wire frame construction technique was used.

PLATE 118. Wire frame, canvas covered Swan made by Manny Haywood of Kill Devil Hill, North Carolina. Haywood used glass eyes in his Swan decoys.

SOUTH CAROLINA

Up to now on books and few periodicals have paid much attention to decoys from South Carolina. This omission is understandable when you consider how few documented South Carolina decoys have been found and added to private collections. On the other hand it is difficult to understand once you have so far been uncovered, for they are striking in beauty, style and size.

The origin of these decoys is still a bit hazy, but so far research in the area indicates that a family from around Georgetown, South Carolina, named Cains is responsible for some of them. There were at least two Cains brothers, Hucks and Saynay Cains and possibly a third, Ball who produced the decoys. One of them is known to have worked for Bernard Baruch on his plantation, Hobcaw Barony. Indeed some decoys attributed to the Cains brothers bear Baruch's brand "BMB."

The most handsome of these decoys have an unmistakable style about them. The head and neck of the Mallards are gracefully carved in what is described as a "snakey neck" or "swan neck" with elongated bills and carved eyes. The head and neck are carved from one piece of wood and the body is of solid one-piece construction. Usually made of Tupelo gum or cypress, they have raised wing carving and, if you view just about any of them from above, you will note a distinctive heart shape formed by the wing carving.

Some of the decoys, particularly Black Ducks, are hollow bodied and often have glass eyes. It should be noted here that it appears some of the Mallard decoys to have been repainted as Black Ducks, and vice versa.

Once you have had the opportunity to personally examine these particular South Carolina decoys you will have no problem knowing that they are valuable. Collector value range is $3000 to $10,000 with a few going much higher at auctions.

PLATE 119. Hen Mallard decoy attributed to Hucks Cains. The grace, beauty and style of carving of this South Carolina decoy is unsurpassed. As are all the South Carolina decoys, this one is painted with much detail in dull muted colors.

PLATE 120. This Mallard drake is the mate to the hen in Plate 119. The wing carving of these decoys, when viewed from above result in the heart shape characteristic of the Cains Mallards. The numerous more or less vertical marks on the body are the result of wrapping the anchor line around the decoy during storage and transport.

PLATE 121. This rather strange looking hen Mallard is attributed to Hucks Cains. It is speculated that this decoy represents one of the earliest attempts at decoy making by the Cains brothers. The narrow portion of the back is obviously made to facilitate anchor line storage.

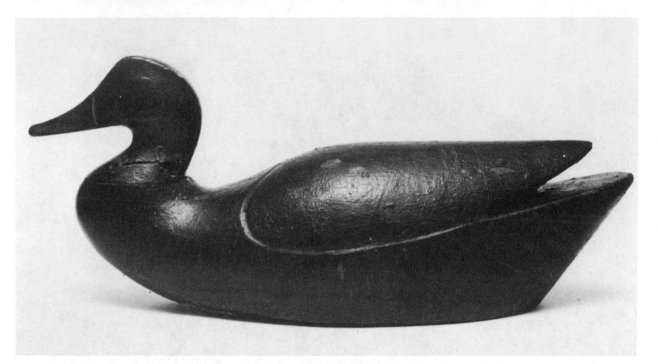

PLATE 122. This swimming or feeding Black Duck is attributed to the Cains brothers because of the unmistakable heart shape formed by the wing carving. This decoy probably represents mid-range in the evolution of Cains Brothers decoy making. Although it is not clear in the photograph, this decoy has no eye representation.

PLATE 123. Although most of the decoys are carved with raised wings, this Mallard drake is referred to as the "raised wing" variety.

PLATE 124. A hollow-body Black Duck. It has glass eyes and the two-piece hollow body is joined at a point above the waterline.

PLATE 125. This is a bottom view of the Black Duck in Plate 124, showing the "BMB" brand of Bernard M. Baruch. So far all the decoys with this brand have been hollow bodied.

PLATE 126. This Ball (Bob?) Cains decoy shot from above shows a defintite heart shape. This heart shape resulting from the raised wing carving is a typical characteristic of Cains Brothers birds.

PLATE 127. Blue Wing Teal attributed to Ball Cains. This decoy can be considered fairly rare because it is the only species other than Black Ducks and Mallards that have been attributed to the Cains Brothers. It is rather elaborately painted, using the scratch feather technique. There are only four of these presently known to be in private collections. The eyes are glass hat pins.

A Mallard drake
by South Carolina maker
Hucks Cains.

This hen Mallard was made by
Hucks Cains of South Carolina.

A drake Mallard from South
Carolina. This particular decoy
illustrates what is known as the
"raised wing" model by collectors of
South Carolina decoys attributed to
the Cains brothers.

This is a typical Barnegat Bay area calling Wood Duck drake. The maker of this two piece hollow white cedar decoy is not known.

Widgeon drake by Lloyd Johnson. This New Jersey decoy has a flat bottom and glass eyes.

Drake Widgeon made by Miles Hancock of Chincoteague, Virginia

This sleeper Wood Duck drake is from the Barnegat Bay area. It is a hollow body decoy made in the two piece method typical of the school. The carver is not known.

A drake Widgeon made by Mason's Decoy Factory in the Premier Grade.

This decoy was made by John Dawson of the Delaware River school. This drake Widgeon is a very good example of a bird from the school.

Mint condition hen and drake Pintails by Lem and Steve Ward. Extremely fine paint jobs are apparent on these classic 1936 models by the Ward Brothers.

A Pintail made by Charles "Shang" Wheeler about 1932. This very nice bird has much original paint, glass eyes, carved mandibles and face carving. The body is comb feather painted and the tail was fashioned from a piece of sheet copper.

An Ed Phillips drake Pintail. A solid body decoy with carved eyes and scratch feather painting. A beautifully carved and painted decoy by this Cambridge, Maryland commercial carver.

A Blue Wing Teal drake from the coast of Maine. This very small decoy was made in the 1920's or earlier but the identity of the maker is not known presently.

This pair of decoys
was made by the Mason's Decoy Factory.
They are Detroit Grade decoys
in the Blue Wing and Green Wing Teal species.

A two piece hollow body Brant decoy made by Ira
Hudson of Chincoteague, Virginia.

A very nice Ira Hudson Black Duck. Although it
doesn't have his typical "banjo tail" when you
examine this bird you can easily see his typical "flute
carving" in the tail.

This Redhead drake was made by the H. A. Stevens
Decoys company of Weedsport, New York. The very
nicely formed, flattish body and paddle tail arc
typical of these factory decoys.

This nice Canada Goose was made by Ed Phillips of Cambridge, Maryland. Made as a "watch Gander" it is scratch feather painted and has a sheet lead ballast weight.

This is a Red Breasted Merganser made by the Wildfowler company. It bears the typical round brand or logo with the Quogue, Long Island location in it.

A Mason's Decoy Factory Challenge Grade drake Merganser in very good condition.

A hollow body
Canada Goose
made by Nathan Cobb.

Hooded Merganser drake
made by Ira Hudson of
the Virginia Eastern
Shore school of carvers.
This decoy illustrates the
"football body" and
"banjo tail" often used
by him.

Red Breasted Merganser
from the Maine school.
The carving and con-
struction details on this
decoy are typical of
Maine. It has an inletted
head and is strikingly
similar to that of decoys
by Gus Wilson but the
painting is more sophisticated than that normally
associated with Wilson's
products.

A Preier Grade drake
Canvasback made by the
Mason's Decoy Factory.

A Ward Brothers drake
Canvasback in original paint.
Sometimes known as the
"Classic '36", it is carved from
solid cedar and sports glass
eyes.

An exceptionally nice Ira
Hudson drake Canvasback
decoy. Note the scalloped
breast feather painting and
"banjo tail" frequently used
by Hudson.

LOUISIANA

Commerical makers produced thousands upon thousands of decoys, running the gamut from crude chunks of wood, decoys painted as if for a carnival midway to superb highly detailed and beautifully painted birds. It seems that everybody and his brother were making decoys. Louisiana makers probably produced a wider variety of species of wildfowl decoys than any other single region in the United States. It is therefore next to impossible to provide the collector with anything more than the broadest generalizations in describing any common characteristics for Louisiana decoys.

There are between fifteen and twenty makers from the Louisiana area that are most popularly collected, but to further complicate the identification and valuation problems, the majority of these decoys reside in just a small number of private collections, most of which belong to Louisiana collectors and, further, there is precious little trade data for the decoys are seldom put on public sale.

A few of the better known makers are: Victor Alfonso, Adam Ansardi, Xavier Bourg, Marc Alcide Comardelle, Jack and Robert Couret, William Duet, Gaston Isadore, Dewey Pertuit, Remie Ange Roussel, Jr., Nick Trahan, Nicole Vidacovich, Clovis "Cadis" Vizier, Mark Whipple and the products of the loose partnership of three men who worked cooperatively: Charles Joefrau, Mitchel LaFrance and George Frederick.

In the last edition of this book I gave the Louisiana carvers short schrift by saying that a hazardous guess might place their value at $100-200.00 for the average block. At the time most collectors didn't realize the value and collectibility of the Louisiana decoy and there was little trade data available. If you glance at the price ranges below, it will be obvious to you that the Louisiana carvers have finally gotten the credit they so richly deserve.

The decoys in the accompanying photographs are by the members of the group of popularly collected Louisiana Carvers.

If you have an interest in collecting decoys from Louisiana, it is strongly recommended that you obtain two books. **Decoys of the Mississippi Flyway** by Alan G. Haid has a large, excellent section of photographs of Louisiana decoys; and **Louisiana Duck Decoys** by Charles W. Frank Jr.

Value Ranges for Louisiana Decoys

Marc Alcide Comardelle	$1000-3000
Dewey Pertuit	$100-300
Remie Ange Roussel, Jr	$500-1000
Nicole Vidacovich	$400-2000
Clovis "Cadis" Vizier	$500-1500
Marc Whipple	$300-1000

PLATE 128. A drake Mallard made by Nick Trahan of Lake Arthur, LA. Made of cypress in solid body type with a rooty looking head and upswept tail, this is not a particularly good overall example of his decoys but the shape of the body is typical. His heads were usually rendered much nicer than this one.

PLATE 129. A very nice Bluewing Teal drake by Xavier Bourg from Larose, Louisiana. Solid body with well carved raised wings and tack eyes.

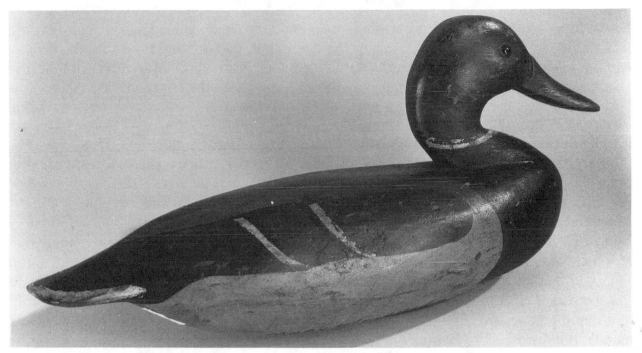

PLATE 203. A Mallard Drake made by Marc Whipple of Bourg, Louisana. c. 1940.

PLATE 205. A very good example of a Green Winged Teal by the Mitchell LaFrance, Charles Joefrau and George Frederick trio. Glass eyes, raised wing carving and nicely painted. c. 1930.

ILLINOIS RIVER

The Illinois River school boasts some of the nicest hollow body working decoys to be found in the country. The norm was to construct them in two pieces that were hollowed out and then joined at a point above the waterline. They were carved realistically with much fine bill and face detail. Some of them even have hollow necks and heads. Just about all have glass eyes. Frequently the commerical makers would have ballast weights made for them with their names cast into the strip lead weight surface, making their products easily identified if the original weight is present.

Most of the decoys have a rounded semi-"V" bottom. Many of them have been found with a coat of shellac or varnish. It is theorized that they felt, because the waters they hunted in were usually muddy or murky, that an orange shellac made them more visible to the live bird.

The Mallard decoy is the most commonly found species in the area for that was the dominant bird in the Mississippi Flyway.

Painting was very realistic with the comb feather painting technique frequently applied.

There were at least 140 carvers in the Illinois River school, from Beardstown to Joliet but, among them all one man, Robert Elliston (1849-1915) has been credited by some experts as having originated what is today known as the Illinois River style of decoy making. He started making them about 1880 and it is thought that he made several thousand before his death in 1915. He fashioned them from white pine in two halves, hollowing each out and joining them so that the joint would be above the waterline when floating. Heads were generally very sloped down to a detailed carved bills. Eyes were glass and placed anatomically correct on his earlier decoys. Later he began placing the eyes. His bodies were made flat-backed, narrow at the shoulders and rear ending in a flat paddle-type tail. Painted by Elliston's wife Catherine, they exhibit beautiful accuracy. She used fine brush and comb in wet paint methods to render the feathers. She was obviously quite accomplished. As with typical examples from this school, they were made with long lead keel weights, often with the weight manufacturer's name and "The Elliston Decoy" stamped or cast into it.

Bert Graves (1887-1956) was another master of the Illinois River school. He made decoys from the late 1920's to the early 1940's. That he was influenced by Elliston is a foregone conclusion. Like Elliston, he placed glass eyes high on the head. As a matter of fact, his early decoys very much emulated Elliston's. His bodies were a little thicker and have a rounded back. It is known that Elliston's wife Catherine painted Graves' decoys after her husband died. Graves' early decoys painted by her are considered the most desirable although the later ones, painted by Graves' sister-in-law are also quite nice.

Charles B. Walker (1876-1954) of Princeton, Illinois worked as a house painter and only made decoys part-time. It is thought that he made fewer than five hundred in his lifetime. His output was largely Mallard drakes and hens though other species such as Pintails have shown up. His works are fine examples of decoy making. The breasts on his decoys do not protrude as much as those more typical of this school of carvers, but are rather flattened. They are all hollow, two-piece white pine in construction. Some are found with carved wing details. Some have round bottoms while others have the typical flat bottoms. His weights were not the typical lead keel type, but rather comprised two pieces. The paint patterns are excellent, rendering individual feathers by brush on the earlier mosdels and later the combing method was utilized sometimes even combining the two methods. Most of his decoys were made for the Princeton Game and Fish Club at Goose Pond.

Some other carvers from the Illinois School are: Oscar Alford, Beardstown; Glen J. Cameron, Chillicothe; Anton Chiado, Granville; Thomas Chiado, Spring Valley; Walter Dawson, Putnam; Leonard Doren, Pekin; Harold Haertel, Dundee; George Kessler, Pekin; Charles Ruggles, Henry; Charles Schoenheider, Peoria and Forest J. Stiles, Savannah.

Value Ranges for Illinois River Decoys

Robert Elliston
  Range for average decoys $300-1000
  Range for exceptional decoys $1000-3000
  Range for extraordinary decoys $3000-10,000
Bert Graves $300-2500
Charles Perdew $1000-5000*
Charles B. Walker $1000-6000

These ranges are all for quite good condition decoys.

PLATE 130. An Illinois River Mallard drake decoy made by J. Fred Mott Sr. around 1898. It is a two-piece hollow body bird with tack eyes and a shelf carving to receive the head/neck. Mott, Sr. was from Pekin, Illinois. Note the strip weight typical of Illinois River decoys.

*Some will go lower and a few will bring in excess of $5000.

PLATE 131. This Illinois River decoy is a drake Mallard made by Perry Wilcoxen of Liverpool, Illinois. Typical two-piece hollow body construction with shelf carving.

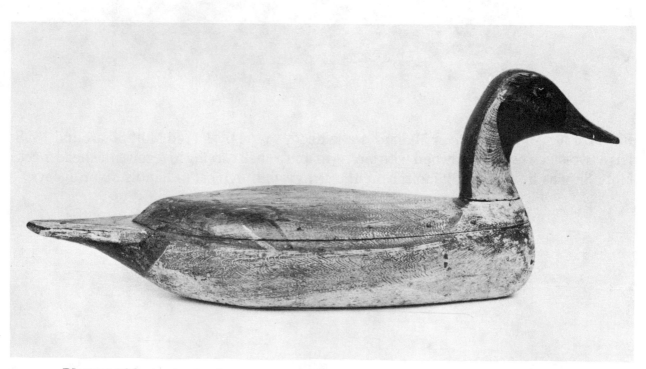

PLATE 132. A nicely shaped Illinois River drake Pintail. Maker unknown.

PLATE 133. Front view of the above Illinois River Pintail showing the thin head and unusual boat-like shape of the body. A very gracefully shaped decoy overall.

PLATE 134. Pintail Duck made by William T. Shaw of Macon, Illinois. Quite typical Illinois River decoy with glass eyes, two-piece hollow body and strip lead ballast weight. The "S" brand visible in the photo was used by Shaw to identify his products. Note the tail carving detail.

PLATE 135. The maker of this Illinois River Scaup drake is not known, but it is another nice example of decoys from the School. It has a typical strip lead weight that bears the inscription "Raymond Lead Company." This company was located in Chicago, Illinois.

130

MICHIGAN

Decoys from this school comprise two types. One type was made for hunting in the heavy waters of the Great Lakes and the other are those made for use in more calm waters and shallow marshes.

The Great Lakes decoys were made large with hollow bodies and big keels. They were generally hollowed out from the bottom and closed up with bottom boards. There are lots of unusual keels to be found on Michigan decoys some of them being downright ingenious. The other type are constructed in the same manner but are usually smaller in scale, lack the large heavy keels and use a very thin bottom board. By the time decoy making had worked its way this far West from the Atlantic seaboard, it was about 1880. Makers of this part of the country had the experience of their Eastern predecessors from which to draw on, many sources for fine materials and good tools available to work with. The band saw and glass eyes are two good examples of this. It is therefore no surprise that the decoys of the Mid-West are for the most part very finely made and finished. Just about all decoys from the region have good quality glass eyes. Most are hollow body types with bottom boards, but there are some very nice solid body birds to be found as well. Some makers also used cork in fashioning bodies and mounted them on bottom boards for stability and durability.

As a whole the decoys of the region are beautifully constructed and painted. The collector would do well to concentrate his efforts in the whole region including Michigan, the St. Clairs Flats, Illinois River, etc. There are probably quite a few decoys as yet not found and there were a few makers who are known to have produced literally thousands of them in their combined carving careers.

Ken Anger (1905-1961) of Dunnville, Ontario may or may not belong with the listing of the Michigan makers. In fact William Mackey listed him as a carver in the New York School in his book **American Bird Decoys**, copyright 1965. The fact is even though he lived and worked in Ontario, much closer to Toronto than Detroit, his blocks are much more similar to those of the Detroit makers than those made of those of Toronto carvers. Furthermore they are quite similar to those of Detriot makers Ben Schmidt and Neil Smith.

Anger used a rasp extensively in fashioning his decoys and developed the technique to such a fine art that when combined with his painting he was able to achieve a realistic soft feather-like texture. It is his trademark. He was so adept at it that collectors have dubbed him the "Raspmaster." Most of his decoys will be found made of two pieces of hollowed out blocks of red cedar joined by glue and two screws. They are mostly flat bottomed with heads carved from basswood and attached to the body by a screw from below. They exhibit nicely rendered wing carving. There are two differnt styles of Angers to be found. His early (pre-mid 1930's) style was a low and gracefully flattened body while the examples made after that have a higher, fatter look to them. They were made to float higher in the water than the older style. The other characteristics, however, remained the same. The decoy in Plate 141-A on page 137 represents an example of the older style.

Value Ranges for Michigan Carvers:
Ben Schmidt $250-1000
Ken Anger $500-2000*
Walter Strubling $300-600

*A few have brought mid four figure prices.

PLATE 136. This beautifully constructed and painted c. 1925 Canvasback drake was made by Walter Strubling of Marine City, Michigan. It is surprisingly light relative to its large size and heavy looking construction. It is hollow bodied with a 5/8″ bottom board and has a very large swing type keel. This keel is very like the swinging keels designed for ease of trailering some small to medium sailboats so common today. The bottom board and keel are attached by means of countersunk brass marine screws. It has glass eyes, fine head and bill carving details and a thick heavy well executed paint pattern. Made for hunting in heavy water such as might be encountered often in the Great Lakes.

PLATE 137. A bottom view of the decoy shown in Plate 136 with the swing keel extended as it would be when floating.

PLATE 138. A Black Duck made by Ben Schmidt of Detroit, Michigan. Slightly smaller than the Strubling Canvasback in Plate 136 this decoy could serve double duty as a big water decoy because of its fairly sizable keel but it was likely made for use in more shallow water and marshes at the edge of the lakes and even in the smaller bodies of water such as Lake St. Clair. This decoy like just about all decoys made by Ben Schmidt has a solid body, glass eyes, and very good raised wing carving details. Schmidt used a very unique method of making feather representations on the bodies of his birds. He shaped his own tool for stamping crescent shaped feather details into the bodies. Some hollow body Schmidt decoys are found though the majority are solid.

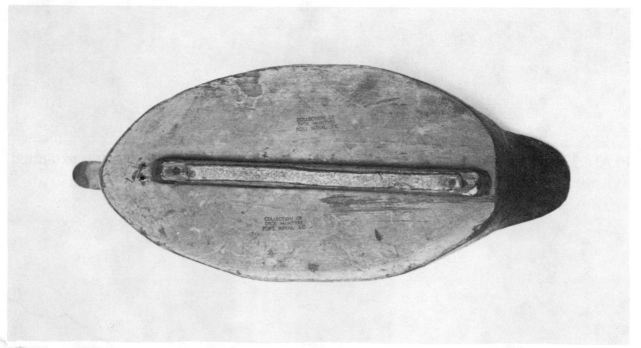

PLATE 139. This bottom view of the Schmidt Black Duck in Plate 138 illustrates the typical keel and strip lead weight be used.

PLATE 140. A hen Canvasback attributed to Ben Schmidt of Detroit.

PLATE 141. Black Duck from Detroit by Neil Smith (friend and student of Ben Schmidt). NES brand. Had a keel at one time full length of flat bottom, solid body; glass eyes; nice bill and face carving; raised wing. Same stamped feather technique developed by Schmidt. c. 1952.

PLATE 37. This solid body Black Duck decoy was made by Ken Anger of Dunnville, Ontario, Canada. Dunnville is located on the far northeastern shore of Lake Erie. It is quite close to Buffalo, New York, but Anger's style seems more like those of the Michigan School. Nevertheless, William Mackey in his book **American Bird Decoys**, places Anger in the New York School. His mastery of the rasp in imparting a beautiful feather texture to his decoys earned him the nickname, "The Raspmaster." (New York State School)

ST. CLAIR FLATS
Mount Clemons and Toronto Schools

For the most part decoys from the banks of St. Clair Flats are very light, well constructed flat-bottom, hollow-body birds with thin bottom boards (some as thin as 1/4 inch). Some even boast hollow necks and heads. They are finely sanded and finished, sporting glass eyes. There were many fine lowheads and sleepers made in the area.

Lake St. Clair is on the United States and Canadian border with the border running north/south through the lake. There are, therefore, American and Canadian carvers in the school. Serious collectors divide the St. Clair Flats into two separate schools, the Toronto School and the Mount Clemons School. The accompanying photographs are of decoys by makers from both sides of the lake. The differences are definite but subtle and not within the purview of this basic guide.

Canadian carvers were frequently given short shrift until ten or twelve years ago. They were apparently particularly adept at carving Canada Geese decoys (that probably should not be a surprise), but they carved many other species also. A particularly noted carver from Toronto was George Warin. A boat builder and commerical decoy maker, he fashioned several styles of Canadas both solid and hollow-bodied, but also carved Blacks, Bluebills, Canvasbacks, Redheads, Mallards, Pintails and Ringnecks. These were usually in the style of typical St. Clair Flats carvers. They are characterized by a finely carved bill, but with no details carved in the bills. They were exquisitely painted with fine detail. Many will be found marked "G & J. Warin Makers Toronto" or "G. & J. Warin Builders." The J. is his brother who was a partner in the boat building business. It is generally held that James had little or nothing to do with the decoy business. It is thought that there were about 2000 decoys made in the years 1870 to 1900.

Another Toronto maker of note was Tom Chambers (1860-1948). He managed the marsh for the St. Clair Shooting Company from 1900 to 1930. Like Warin he made a very stylish Canada Goose decoy as well as many others. Also like Warin, made some with solid bodies, but most are in the St. Clair Flats style. The majority of his decoys were Canvasbacks and Redheads, but you can find most of the other species common to the area. They are characterized by detail carving of the bill with diamond-shaped nostrils. Some of the later decoys he made are found with "Thos. Chambers Maker" on the bottom.

Some other St. Clair Flats makers are Robert C. McGaffey, Ontario; David Ward, Toronto; William Finkel, St. Clair Flats; Zeke McDonald, McDonald Island, Mich.; Danny Scriven, Detroit; Phineas Reeves and sons, Charles and John, Port Rowan, Ontario; Davey Nichols, Smith's Falls, Ontario; Tobin Meldrum, Fair Haven, Mich.; Frank Schmidt, Detroit and John R. Wells, Toronto.

Value Ranges for Some St. Clair Flats Carvers:

Thomas Chambers	$750-3500
Ralph Reghi	$200-500
George Warin	$750-1500

PLATE 142. A very nice Redhead drake by Canadian St. Clair Flats maker Thomas Chambers. A very typical decoy from this school, it is a flat-bottom hollow body bird with a thin bottom board. It has glass eyes and excellent detailed mandible carving. The carved diamond-shape nostrils is an identifying characteristic of Thomas Chambers decoys.

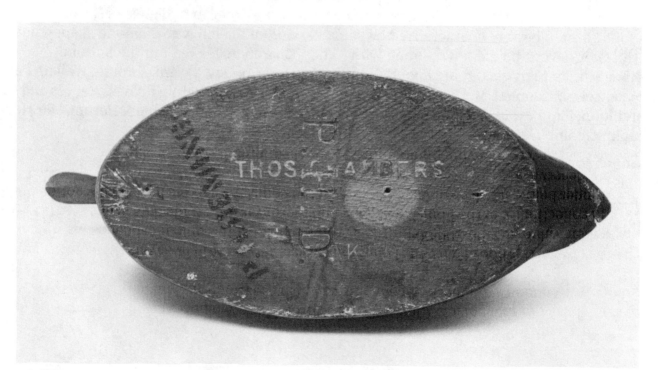

PLATE 143. View of the bottom of the Thomas Chambers Redhead in Plate 142, showing various brands. The important one to note here is "THOS CHAMBERS." If you look close toward the lower side in the photo of the bottom, you can see the "K" that is part of the word "MAKER."

PLATE 144. This is a very nice and very old Canvasback by Tobin Meldrum (Meldren in some references) of Fairhaven, Michigan, on the far northern shore of Lake St. Clair. Typical hollow body decoy with thin bottom board and glass eyes. This decoy would delight any collector of folk art as well as the collector of St. Clair Flats School decoys.

PLATE 145. A very small hollow-body bottom board St. Clair Flats decoy with glass eyes and nice bill and face carving. Very little original paint left on the decoy whose maker is unknown.

PLATE 146. A St. Clair Flats drake Redhead by Thomas Chambers.

PLATE 147. This is a solid body, glass eye drake Canvasback by Ralph Reghi. This particular decoy was used on the St. Clair Flats but differs from the norm. It represents a smaller group of carvers that made their birds in the Mount Clemons style. Mount Clemons is just north of Detroit on the northwestern side of Lake St. Clair.

PLATE 148. This is a later Tom Schroeder drake Redhead. His earlier hollow-body birds were typical St. Clair Flats decoys. This one is in the same style but is a solid body composition with a wooden head.

WISCONSIN

With the exception of factory-made decoys, there were few commercial makers in the Wisconsin School. Most of the decoys of the area were made by the individual hunters for themselves and perhaps a few for friends. There were nevertheless many, many fine decoys made in Wisconsin.

Decoys from this school are generally oversize renditions of diving ducks species. They are usually found in solid-body construction, but there are some very nice hollow-body examples to be found as well. Whatever the construction technique, they all usually have exaggerated body features such as big, long necks and hump backs. Most sport glass eyes.

Paint styles or patterns are usually very similar to factory birds widely used in the Midwest.

There are many makers from this school that turned out nice blocks, but there are two who stand out in quality and numbers fashioned: August "Gus" Moak (1852-1942) of Tustin and Frank G. Strey (1890-1966). Oshkosh.

Moak's birds are hollow cedar and he utilized bottom boards that were slightly convex. The bodies were the typical hump back and necks were long. The heads are distinctive in that there is a deep vee carved separating the bills from the foreheads. There are very obvious carved nostrils and mandibles.

Decoys made by Frank Strey are big, solid blocks. The cheeks are pronounced as the result of his carving out elongated recesses for the recessed eyes. In later years he didn't carve the cheeks quite so deep and he had begun to use a rasp to give the surface a textured look.

Value Ranges for Wisconsin Decoys
August "Gus" Moak (1852-1942) $500-1000
Frank Strey (1890-1966) $200-600

PLATE 149. This hen Canvasback is from Wisconsin, but the maker is not presently known. It is quite similar to those made by August Moak and Joseph Sieger of the Wisconsin School.

PLATE 150. A drake Canvasback, mate to the hen in Plate 149. Both have glass eyes and paint patterns similar to factory-made decoys of the Midwest. Both exhibit the hump backs and long necks discussed in the accompanying text. It must have proved quite a problem to transport and deploy more than six or eight of these large, heavy solid body decoys. Both show much repair, lending evidence to their susceptibility to damage in handling.

PLATE 151. A beautiful little pair of Greenwing Teals from Wisconsin. The maker of these decoys is not known. They are two-piece hollow body decoys with glass eyes and finely carved face and bill and feather details. A lot of Wisconsin birds are found with small brass or copper tags with the owner's name and address inscribed.

143

PLATE 152. A c. 1930 drake Redhead made by Frank Strey of Oshkosh, Wisconsin. Strey's decoys were heavy over-sized solid body birds. They generally have good face and bill carving details although the amount and attention to this carving diminished as the years went by. The bodies also have varying degrees of rasp work. Glass eyes and flat bottoms complete the list of typical characteristics of the birds from the hands of this Wisconsin School carver.

Shelburne Museum

PLATE 204. Another Frank Strey. This a very nice c. 1920 Scaup Drake exhibiting all the typical Strey characteristics.

PACIFIC COAST

Although not foolproof, of course, the type of wood used to fashion a decoy is a good clue to decoys from the West Coast or Pacific Flyway. The wood of choice for most makers of the area was redwood. Often they used ponderosa pine for heads also. Another good way to identify a West Coast decoy is by species. For instance, the Pacific Coast Black Brant has a different plumage pattern than that of the Brant that migrates through the eastern flyways.

Generally the hand-carved decoys of the Pacific Coast are solid bodied and sport tack eyes. Many have a similar look about them. There are many notable exceptions to these generalities as elsewhere. Some of the makers who worked after 1900 (some still carving) were very talented. The beautiful late 1930's Mallards, Canvasback and Teals of Harry L. Cook are good examples of this.

The Pacific Coast School as we use it here encompasses the whole of the United States West Coast from northern California to Washington. About twenty percent of the pre-World War II decoys found in the region are hand-carved as described in the preceding paragraphs. The remaining eighty percent of the decoys found are factory-made being primarily Masons.

Perhaps the dean of the Pacific coast decoy makers was Richard Ludwig "Fresh Air Dick" Jantzen of the San Francisco area. In his twenty-odd years of carving he produced thousands of decoys. He carved just about all the species hunted. His blocks are almost always characterized by slightly hump-backed bodies of redwood with distinctly carved wings and tail (see Plate 154). The heads may or may not be mounted on a shelf, but all are puffy cheeked, have glass eyes and nicely carved bills. The bodies are found both solid and hollow. Unfortunately for the collector his style was so respected that many other carvers copied it.

Horace Crandall (1892-1969), Westwood, California is another carver of note in the Pacific Coast school. His decoys differ from most of the other products of the region in that they were very slender and graceful, almost to the point where they might be considered elegant. They had upswept tails and a fragile slim neck. Toward the end of his carving career he began fashioning his decoys with carved upsweeping wing similar to those of Jantzen. The bodies were solid pine.

Some other carvers in the region worthy of note are: Frank Bay (1896-1980) and brother, Jack Bay (1882-1941) of Astoria, Oregon; Charles Bergman (1856-1946), also of Astoria and Luigi Andreucetti (1898-1978) of the Sacremento, California area.

There is a super book about the carvers of this region that any collector of west coast decoys should have. It is **Wildfowl Decoys of the Pacific Coast** by Michael R. Miller and Frederick W. Hanson. It is listed in the Recommended Books section on pages 35-39.

Value Ranges for Pacific Coast Decoys
Richard Ludwing "Fresh Air Dick" Jantzen $750-5000*
Harry L. Cook $200-650
Horace Crandall $750-2000

*A few have brought much more.

PLATE 153. The maker of this Pacific Coast Black Brant is not known. It is an excellent representation of West Coast decoys of the species. It is solid body constructed of redwood, as tack eyes, and is rigged with line ties fore and aft. It is a 1920's decoy from the Northern Coast of California.

PLATE 154. This is a hen Pintail made by Dick "Fresh Air" Jantzen of California. His birds represent some of the really nice decoys to be found on the West Coast. This particular one was hollowed out by drilling out through the breast area.

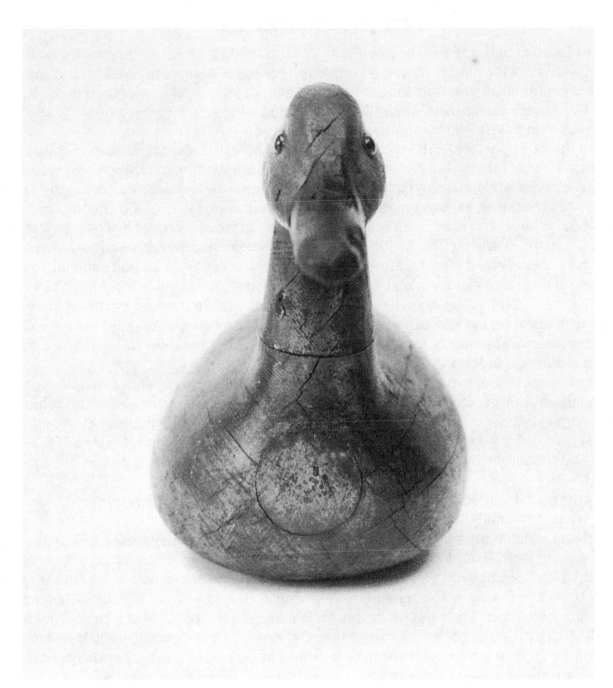

PLATE 155. A front view of the above Jantzen Pintail showing the plug where the decoy was drilled out from. Jantzen did not always use this method.

FACTORY DECOYS

During the last half of the 1800's the popularity of sport hunting increased dramatically. This coupled with the appearance of the market hunter, his requisite large rigs of decoys and the advent of the duplicating lathe made it economically feasible for the establishment of factories for the commerical manufacture of decoys. There were established hundreds of operations, a few of which became large and successful. There were also several small operations to achieve success.

The use of the word "factory" can be misleading as used here. It does indeed describe large operations such as Mason's Decoy Factory, but here we are also including any commercial operation location devoted to the manufacture of wooden decoys in which the duplicating lathe is an integral part of their production, or the production, lathe or no, was on an assembly line basis. This latter could encompass many, many makers, but only those who have been routinely accepted as factory decoys by collectors are included. Most of these have been accepted as "factories" by virtue of extensive commercial advertising of the decoys.

Factory made decoys made by the most well known companies were all quite similar to each other. Excepting the Stevens and Victor Animal Trap Companies, who came along before Mason's Decoy Factory, it appears that most of the better known factory decoys made were influenced by Mason products. Mason and probably many others would, however, make atypical decoys on special order but their regular lines all performed their tasks in pretty much the same manner in most conditions. Therefore a small degree of standardization was practiced, albeit by accident.

Manufacturing operations were in a position to make innovations in decoys not practical to hand makers. Some of the innovations such as the folding tin shorebird decoys were successful and some were little more than comical. A decoy that flapped its wings was once patented; a dubious achievement at best.

The metal bodied decoys with wood bottom boards and the folding tin shorebirds had appeared by the mid-1860's and rubber decoys arrived about 1867. There were even some "honking" decoys produced by factories.

The art of the manufactured wooden decoy, however, was carried to its highest form by the early factories and this is what they finally concentrated their efforts on.

The collector can encounter factory decoys just about anywhere for they were made by the thousands (especially around Detroit) and shipped to just about all points of the compass. A notable exception is New England. There seems to be a shortage of factory made decoys in that part of the country. Conjecture leads us to think the reason is the reputation New Englanders have to being handy, educated in fine craftsmanship, industrious and possessing innate "Yankee ingenuity." In short, they probably thought "Anything they can do, we can do better" and proceeded to make their own, shunning store bought decoys.

While hunting for factory decoys it might be judicious to keep in mind another theoretical possibility. It would not be unreasonable to think that some employees of factories carried their vocation home and made decoys in home workshops. There were many talented people working in these factories (especially painters) and there would be nothing to prevent them from making decoys. It is most reasonable to assume some of them might have produced birds that were almost, if not completely, identical to the factory product. I can't pretend to advise you what to do or think about this possibility but am compelled to pint it out to you.

The new wildfowl laws of 1918 struck a fatal blow to the manufacturing companies, and factory after factory went out of business almost overnight. The laws eliminated the market hunters, thus their huge demand for decoys simply vanished.

J.N. DODGE

Jasper N. Dodge (1829-1909) of Detroit, Michigan, went into business about 1883, when he bought an existing decoy making operation owned by George Peterson. Peterson had been in business since 1873. The Peterson products were very fine, usually solid body birds with glass eyes. Although Dodge didn't use Peterson's original patterns, he did utilize many of the existing techniques. His were also generally solid bodied but, like Peterson, he also manufactured some hollow decoys in the St. Clair Flats style.

Early Dodge decoys had unusual eyes. The eye hole was drilled out and a tack placed in the hole, resulting in slightly recessed tack eyes that appeared very much like glass eyes. Later he adopted the glass eyes. There is usually evidence of Dodge's extensive use of putty filler where the neck joins the body. Dodge also carried on the breast swirl style of painting developed by Peterson. This swirl style was later used extensively by the Mason's Decoy Factory in Detroit.

Dodge advertised that he would make decoys "...after any model furnished without extra charge." It is therefore possible to find many different types, styles and species made by the company. He went out of business in 1908, but there has been no evidence uncovered to date that he produced decoys past 1905.

Value Ranges for J.N. Dodge Decoys
Merganser and Canada Goose $1000-6000
Other Species $100-750

PLATE 156. A very early original paint Canada Goose by J.N. Dodge. This bird probably dates prior to about 1890. It has great original paint for its age, nice bill carving and the recessed tack eyes discussed in the accompanying text.

PLATE 157. A later model decoy by J.N. Dodge. This hen Scaup has no bill and face carving. Glass eyes were the rule in these later birds, but most significant is the swirl paint pattern on the breast. See text discussion.

EVANS DUCK DECOY COMPANY

Walter Evans (1872-1948) of Ladysmith, Wisconsin, began making decoys in 1921 and continued in business only until 1932 when illness forced him to cease operation. In the beginning the factory consisted of two lathes in his garage. His success was rapid for just a couple of years later he had moved into a large building in Ladysmith and employed a number of people. He offered three different types or grades of decoys in various species. The largest grade, the "Mammoth," was offered only in solid bodies by the other two, the "Standard" and "Competitive" were offered in both solid and hollow bodies. The "Competitive" grade was not sanded but rather left with the ridged lathe blade marks around the body. The others were very nicely sanded and finished.

The hollow bodies were fashioned by two different methods. One is the familiar two-piece hollow body, in two more or less equal halves, but the other method was rather unusual. He would take a solid body and drill a one and one-fourth inch hole through the front of the breast longitudinally into the body. He then plugged the hole in front and finished the bird.

All heads were hand carved and sported quality glass eyes. His method of preparing his decoys for painting was effective, rendering the finish very durable. Many are found today with very good original paint as a result.

The decoys have a Mason look to them and, indeed, it is said that he was inspired to go into the business of decoy making after finding a Mason premier grade Mallard and, being a woodworker by trade, deciding that he could do as well.

Evans frequently rubber stamped the words "Evans Decoy" on the bottom of these flat bottom decoys. This stamp is not always found as he, like most other makers, individuals or factories, wasn't particularly diligent in placing his brand on his products.

Numbers of birds he produced are not known, but a widely circulated photograph of him at work in his shop pictures about 150 Mallard and Canvasback decoys in various stages of completion. With this evidence it can reasonably be assumed that in ten or eleven years he must have produced at least a minimum of one thousand decoys, perhaps many more.

The collection value range for Evans decoys run from $100 to $500.

PLATE 158. A drake Bluebill or Scaup made by the Evans Duck Decoy Company of Ladysmith, Wisconsin. Hollow body with glass eyes.

151

PLATE 159. Front view of the Scaup decoy in Plate 158 showing the plug in the breast. This seals off the 1¼ inch hole made by Evans' unusual method of hollowing out the body of some of his decoys. Discussed in further detail in the accompanying text.

PLATE 160. Bottom view of the Scaup in Plate 159 showing the rubber stamped brand frequently found on Evans decoys.

HERTERS, INC.

Many of the Herters early decoys are desirable to collectors but by far the most highly sought are the Owl and Crow decoys. They made the best Owls of any of the others. Their Owls, for instance, usually exceed one thousand dollars when put up at auction.

The breaks of the Owls were actually made from grizzly bear claws.

Most of their birds found today have solid balsa bodies and cedar heads.

The company is still located in Waseca, Minnesota. The collectible decoys from Herters date around the 1930's and 1940's, with some fairly desirable ones being made in the 1960's.

Herters marketed some birds in the late 1960's and early 1970's under the name "Ancient Wooden Decoys" which were not decoys at all. They were Wood ducks, Mergansers, Mallards, etc., that were flat bottomed, not rigged and not keeled. They were made for decorative purposes only. They are branded "Herters 1893." This is reference only to the year the company was founded.

The collector value range for Herters decoys is $75 to $300.

PLATE 161. A Herters' Great Horned Owl and a Crow. The "V" shape notch in the base of the Owl is made to receive and hold a dead crow decoy, thereby making it look as if the owl had killed it. Owls are deadly enemies of crows and this arrangement ostensibly enraged the crows to attack. The dead Crow decoy is exceedingly rare.

154

PLATE 162. Snuggler Head Canada Goose by Herters', Inc. Balsa body and cedar head.

PLATE 163. Balsa body Coot decoy by Herters', Inc.

MASON'S DECOY FACTORY

Of all the factory made decoys, the ones made by Mason are the most famous. There are more Mason decoys sitting around in living rooms and collections than any other decoys made in the country. They were in Detroit, going into business around 1895 and continuing until 1924. They made five grades of decoys. The best was labelled "Premier," then came "Challenge," "Detroit" grade (called 3 grade Glass Eye by most collectors), 3rd grade Tack Eye, and Fourth Grade. The last three were called "No.1 Glass Eye," "No. 2 Glass Eye" and "No. 3 Painted Eye" respectively by the company. There are other names such as "Challenge Grade Hollow" model which was usually a special order.

Weighs of all sorts are found on Masons, but there was a standard weight used by Mason. They didn't attach them at the factory but shipped them separate in the same box. The buyers had to attach the weight themselves.

Premier Grade Masons had very fine bill and face carving, including a nicely carved nail at the end of the bill. This nail carving was not present on any of the lesser grades. The nail on the Challenge Grade decoys, for instance, was merely painted on.

Premier Grade characteristics are: finely carved bills with the all important **carved** nail representation; two-piece hollow bodies normally, with flat bottoms; glass eyes, and very beautiful paint, including the well known Mason swirl pattern on the breast.

Challenge Grade Masons are characterized by either solid (most of them) or hollow bodies, depending upon how the hunter ordered them; bill carving not nearly so pronounced as on Premier Grades; good paint but also not quite so elaborate as the Premiers; most significantly, a painted black dot to represent the nail, not carved as in Premiers; and glass eyes.

Standard Grade or Detroit Grade Masons have glass eyes; no bill carving at all but details represented by painting. They are all smaller than the Challenge or Premier Grades.

The No. 2 Tack Eye (Mason terminology) is exactly as it says. It is quite nearly the same as the above Standard or Detroit grade but has **tack eyes**.

The No. 3 Painted Eyes is the same as the No. 2 except it has painted eyes as stated in the name. This was the most economical grade in the line.

There are a number of non-standard or atypical Masons about, but most of them were special order decoys.

The Mason style of construction and painting was apparently derived from the earlier products of two earlier Michigan factory type decoys made by George Peterson and his successor Jasper N. Dodge (see page 150.) They were in business in excess of twenty years prior to the Mason Factory.

Value Ranges for Mason Decoys

Merganser, Brant and Canada Goose decoys have all brought far in excess of the value ranges listed here at various auctions, but what is listed here reflects normal averages for decoys in all grades.

Black Duck	$300-1000
Bluebill	$200-800
Blue Wing Teal	$400-1000
Brant	$500-2000
Canada Goose	$500-2000
Canvasback	$300-700
Goldeneye	$200-600
Green Wing Teal	$600-2000
Mallard	$300-1500

PLATE 164. A Mason Premier model Canvasback drake. Two-piece hollow body, swirled breast paint, glass eyes, and fine detailed face and bill carving. If you examine the photo carefully, you can just barely see the **carved** nail at the tip of the bill. This is found only on Mason's Premier grade decoys.

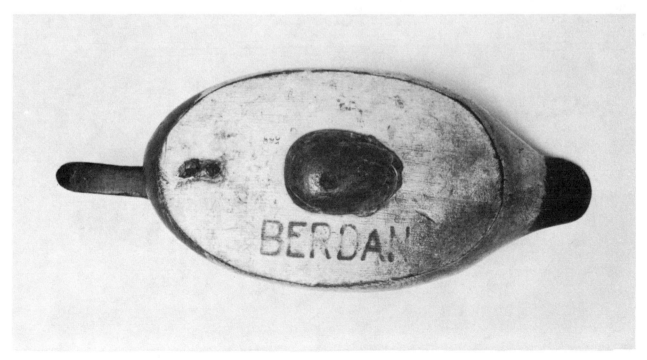

PLATE 165. This bottom view of the Canvasback in Plate 164 shows the typical Mason ballast weight and the brand of the Berdan Gun Club.

PLATE 166. This Mason drake Widgeon decoy is a Premier grade model. It exhibits all the Premier grade characteristics although you may not be able to discern the carved nail in the photograph.

PLATE 167. A hen Broadhill in the Challenge grade by Mason. An unusual Challenge grade hollow body decoy.

PLATE 168. Drake Broadbill mate to the decoy in Plate 167. The Challenge grade painted black dot nail representation is clearly seen on the end of the bill. Hollow body.

PLATE 169. A Mason Standard or Detroit grade Greenwing Teal drake. This decoy is not in exceptional shape but it is a species of Mason decoy not found often.

PLATE 170. Standard or Detroit grade Bluewing Teal drake by Mason's Decoy Factory.

PLATE 171. A Challenge grade Mason Brant is excellent condition. This particular decoy was once the property of the Barron Gun Club. The brand is always applied in two places, on the back and on the left side, as seen in the illustration.

PLATE 172. A Mason Standard or Detroit grade Canvasback hen. This solid body decoy is a special order. The body is unusually long and slender for the typical Detroit grade decoys and the head looks more like Goldeneye heads than Canvasback heads.

PLATE 173. This is the drake Canvasback mate to the hen in Plate 172.

PLATE 174. This Premier grade Mason hen Redhead is a special order decoy. It differs primarily from the typical Permier grade in that the tail is not swept up as is usual. There is an unusual cheek profile. It is a Mason but differs considerably from the norm.

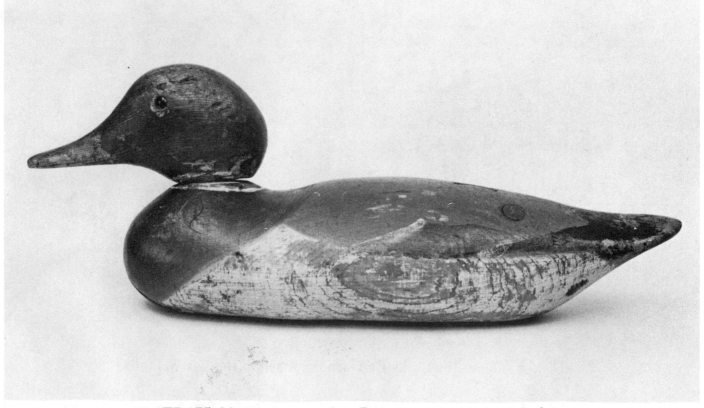

PLATE 175. Mason Standard or Detroit grade Mallard drake.

162

PLATE 176. Challenge grade Mason Black Duck.

PLATE 177. Very nice Standard or Detroit grade Mason Black Duck.

PLATE 178. Challenge grade Mason Brant.

PLATE 179. Pair of Mason's Decoy Factory Teals. Challenge grade.

WILLIAM E. PRATT MANUFACTURING COMPANY

This company was in business from 1920 in Joliet, Illinois. In 1924, when the Mason's Decoy Factory went out of business, Pratt bought out their production line and went into decoy making full time, but the company never approached the quality of Mason's decoys. Most of their decoys exhibit the rough ridging left by the lathe blades. They called this a "feather finish" model, but this was more likely a way to glamorize their lack of sanding and finishing the decoys.

Because Pratt most likely picked up some Mason inventory with the purchase, collectors sometimes find nice Mason bodies with Pratt heads on them.

The decoy in the accompanying Plate 180 is a typical Mason Premier grade pattern, but obviously not nearly so well finished. The other two are better finished, higher quality Pratt products. They offered various degrees of quality over the years until eventually being purchased by the Animal Trap Company (see page 171) Value Range: $100-500.00

PLATE 180. This Bluewing Teal drake is a very good example of the feather finish model made by the William E. Pratt Manufacturing Company. This was apparently their way of saying that they didn't send them. See Victor Animal Trap Company on page 171.

PLATE 181. Drake Mallard attributed to the William E. Pratt company. This one may be a re-head, as the head seems out of proportion for the body. This is not the norm for Pratt decoys.

PLATE 182. A nice Bluewing Teal drake attributed to the William E. Pratt Manufacturing Company.

H.A. STEVENS c. 1880

Harvey A. Stevens lived and worked in Weedsport, New York. He died in 1894 and his brother George W. Stevens apparently carried on for a while, for there have been some found with his initials in the brand.

Stevens decoys were marked "H.A. Stevens, Weedsport, N.Y." by use of stencils, so if you find an original paint model, it should be easy to identify. If you are not so lucky, there are other reliable ways. He almost always manufactured his decoys with an inletted lead weight (poured into a drilled circular hole) and a line tie staple recessed in a similar hole. Tails are paddle type and glass eyes were the rule. Paint was fairly thick and the comb feather technique was used extensively and heads were screwed into the body from the top, resulting hole plugged with a piece of dowel.

The collector value range for Stevens decoys is from $300 to $2000 with a few bringing $2500-$5000.

PLATE 183. This Redhead drake was made by H.A. Stevens. The very nicely formed, flattish body and paddle tail are typical of his factory decoys. Note the comb feather paint pattern.

PLATE 184. Bottom view of the Redhead in Plate 183. The one-inch holes with lead in one for ballast (sometimes more than one is found), and the one forward has a staple for the anchor line tie. Both are characteristic of Stevens decoys. If you look very closely, you can see the remnants of his brand. The "H" and "W" are barely discernible above and between the weight and line tie. This part of the brand "H.A. Stevens, Weedsport, N.Y." Toward the rear end you can see the "S" and "D" from the word "STANDARD."

PLATE 185. An H.A. Stevens Scaup decoy. Note the comb feather painting and the nicely carved mandible details.

PLATE 186. Typical Canvasback drake by H.A. Stevens.

VICTOR ANIMAL TRAP COMPANY

There is much confusion surrounding the products of this company. The reason is the obscure history or evolution of the company.

The best I have been able to discern in researching the company remains confusing. It seems that the Animal Trap Company of America in Lititz, Pennsylvania, purchased the William E. Pratt Manufacturing Company including among other things a decoy making operation. Some time after this purchase the company also obtained two more decoy making operations located in Pascagoula, Mississippi. There apparently was a fire at some point during these various purchases that shut down the Mississippi decoy operations for a period of time, but they did go back into production.

There were various companies making decoys in the Pascagoula area, but the two better known were those of the Victor Company and the Pascagoula Decoy Company whose decoys were sold under the tradename "PADCO." The Victor Company products, when marked, carry the stamp "VICTOR" and later, "ANIMAL TRAP CO. OF MISSISSIPPI, Inc."

Although the paint patterns used by the two different companies were somewhat different from each other, the lathe-turned bodies were almost identical. They are crude looking but nicely shaped and both companies left the ribbed or ridged look imparted by the duplicating lathe blades, ostensibly to give the decoys some representation of feathers. It could just as easily be said that the marks were left to save time and money in the finishing process.

The degree to which the grooves or ribs are apparent was probably due to the type of wood from which the decoys were made. Generally speaking, the harder the wood the more obvious the ribbing.

Heads were attached by wooden dowels, some being left loose for changing head position or transporting them without damage.

Painting was done by spraying, perhaps with some hand work. Hundreds of thousands of these birds were made and sold through several companies' sales catalogs, such as Sears and Roebuck and Montgomery Ward. They became tremendously popular after the end of World War II. They are probably the most commonly found decoys in the country so, unless the decoy from one of these companies is a rarely found type, such as a Teal, chances are the value is going to be less than $100.00, even if found in original paint.

PLATE 187. A Victor Animal Trap Company Mallard drake. Note the ridges around the body that were made by the duplicating lathe blades. It has glass eyes, which is the rule with these birds.

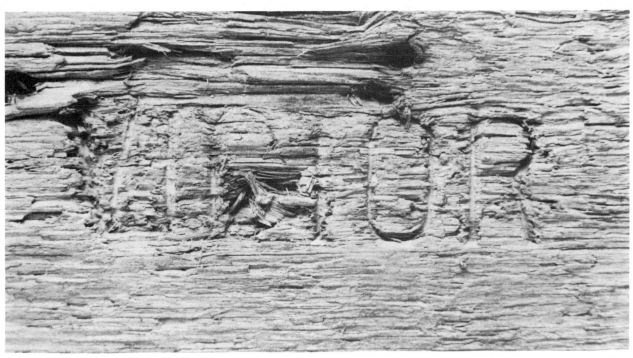

PLATE 188. A close-up photograph of the "VICTOR" brand found on the bottom of the Mallard decoy in Plate 187.

WILDFOWLER DECOYS, INC.

The company began doing business in 1939 in Old Saybrook, Connecticut and is still doing business today in Babylon, Long Island, New York. They can therefore lay legitimate claim to being the oldest operating decoy factory in the United States. The earliest decoys had bodies of white pine and heads of white birch. For the first two years or so the bodies were fashioned by hollowing them out from the bottom and carefully inletting the bottom. This proved to be too tedious and time consuming so they modified the process so that they could simply fit a full bottom board to the hollowed out body. All made after 1941 will exhibit a bottom board. All the decoys will have inletted heads and a keel. Some time shortly after the end of WW II balsa became readily available again and they switched to dense balsa bodies. The pine bodies were still offered, but only on special order. Some sources say that heads may also be found made of cedar and pine.

It is reported that the Old Saybrook factory produced up to 15,000 birds per year in its eighteen years of operation there. There were two grades of decoys available. The best was designated "No. 1" and the second, "No. 2." The difference was the detail in the paint finish. The No. 1 had more feather detail than the No. 2 grade. The No. 1 also had a more smooth finish than did the No. 2 grade. All sported glass eyes.

Many were marked with the stamp (on the bottom) reproduced in the photo reproduced in Plate 194. Notice the complete name, "Old Saybrook...." in the stamp. At some later date the "Old" was dropped from the stamp. Although this attractive stamp makes identification and dating fairly easy, unfortunately many decoys were made without the stamp. It is known that Wilfowler made several thousand decoys for Abercrombie and Fitch without the stamp. It is safe to assume that they made them for resale to other companies as well.

In 1957 the Company was sold to Robert H. "Rab" Staniford and moved to Quogue, New York on Long Island. The brand remained the same but the location on it was changed to "Quogue, L.I.N.Y." (See Plate No. 193) These decoys were still made of dense balsa with the pine heads, however the heads were no longer inletted.

In 1961 the company was sold and moved yet again. It was bought by Charlie Birdsall who moved the operation to the head of Barnegat Bay to Point Pleasant, New Jersey. He changed the location portion of the brand stamp accordingly.

The latest sale was to Amel and Karen Massa in the mid 1970's. It is located in Babylon on Long Island, New York. The collector value range for Wildfowler decoys is from $100 to $500.

PLATE 189. An Atlantic Coast Model Brant decoy made in the Old Saybrook, Connecticut Wildfowler factory. This decoy has a balsa body.

PLATE 190. Redhead drake by Wildfowler Decoys. This bird has a representation of a nail at the end of the bill, not normally found on later models.

PLATE 191. This Wildfowler hen Red Breasted Merganser decoy has glass eyes, a cedar head, and balsa body. It was made in the Quogue, L.I., New York, factory.

PLATE 192. This is a drake Red Breasted Merganser by Wildfowler. It was made in the Quogue, L.I., New York factory and has balsa body, cedar head and glass eyes.

PLATE 193. Closeup photograph of the Wildfowler brand sometimes found on their decoys. This brand remained the same throughout production, with only the factory town location changing. This particular one is from the Quogue, Long Island, factory.

PLATE 194. This Wildfowler brand is from the Old Saybrook, Connecticut factory.

PLATE 195. Wildfowler Decoy Company Black Duck.

PLATE 196. A Canvasback male by Wildfowler. Mint condition, never hunted over.

PLATE 197. A drake Pintail by Wildfowler.

PLATE 198. A hen Scaup made by Wildfowler.

178

PLATE 199. Drake Scaup by Wildfowler. Mate to the hen Scaup in Plate 198.

PLATE 200. A very nice unbranded balsa body Canada Goose made by Wildfowler. Original paint.

COLLECTING DUCK CALLS

A Collector's Guide
to the Identification and Collecting of
American Duck, Goose and
other Wildfowl Calls

By Carl F. Luckey

INTRODUCTION

Over the years I have spent traveling, making new friends and gathering photographs and research material for this book I have noted that many decoy collectors also possess a few duck calls. As a matter of fact, many of the collectors are or were wildfowlers and this addition of other hunting paraphernalia would be a natural adjunct to a nice decoy collection. What ever the reason, I began to note an increasing interest in calls as collectibles and back in mid-1988 I began to look into it. To my surprise I found very little formal written material on call collecting. What I did find was I was not only one who had noted this void in written information for collectors. That year Brian McGrath came out with his fine book **Duck Calls and other Game Calls**, a very interesting and highly useful book for collectors of Reelfoot Lake calls by Russell Caldwell, **Reelfoot Lake, History-Duck Call Makers-Hunting Tales** was released and that Howard Harlan and W. Crew Anderson were close to releasing their incredible book **Duck Calls, an Enduring American Folk Art**. Unlike books on collecting decoys (there are over seventy-five), these three and a few magazine articles represent the body of work so far. They are very good and you should have a copy of each in your library, but as Harlan and Anderson say about information regarding duck calls: *"Some of this story has been lost. Until now, no one thought it important enough to research and write down." In their introduction they have done as I have in my last nineteen books about collectibles. They ask for your input; any information, photographs, old advertising, etc. In short, if you have anything you think they might be interested in, they would like to see it. This has resulted in much more accurate and complete subsequent editions of many of my previous books. I quote them again: **"To that end we view this publication as a beginning, not an end, and we continue to solicit your help."

This small duck call section of this book is in no way an attempt to better the work of those four men. I seriously doubt I could do so in any case. What I have set forth here is, I hope, a basic guide to this particular collecting discipline, a primer if you will. I have made no attempt to produce a comprehensive guide. The basic thrust is for those who might develop an interest in collecting old duck and other game calls. It is not meant to cover the contemporary calls. There is, however, a fundamental problem in trying to eliminate the modern, contemporary call from this work. Many of the old, collectible calls were made by makers who are still working and producing fine calls. In this case the new calls, when possible, will not be included.

The development of the art and science of call making has reached high pinnacles so far. The calling contests and contestants have constantly demanded finer and finer instruments and this has resulted in the high quality, technologically advanced calls produced by makers today. Unbelievably, they are still improving them. The final quality of a call is found, however, in the ability of the hunter to use it. A fine call does not a fine caller make, and used wrong not only lessens your chances at bagging a limit or any birds at all for that matter. Bad calls can at the very least, make friends unhappy and nearby hunters downright angry. The latter have been known to express their dissatisfaction in most unpleasant words and actions and, if you persist in driving the birds away, the former may become the latter, making it very difficult to find hunting companions.

Although quality and versatility of the sounds capable of being made on a call can certainly have a bearing on its collectibility, it is more important with contemporary calls than with the old ones. This is the reason that it is given short shrift in this presentation. Most of the old calls that survived probably were as effective as was needed or required at the time or they probably would not have survived.

Today we still have many makers of fine game calls, but increasingly they are made by mass production. In itself, this is no big deal, neither good nor bad, for the products are generally of good quality else the hunter wouldn't buy or use them. It is lamentable for the hunter, however, for he no longer has the sense of pride and knowledge of the maker that comes with a good, hand-crafted call. A very real problem with these calls is the increasingly widespread tendency to make them so they cannot be taken apart by

*Page 259 **Duck Calls, and Enduring American Folk Art** by Howard Harlan and W. Crew Anderson. Copyright 1988, Harlan Anderson Press
Page xiii. **Duck Calls, and Enduring American Folk Art by Howard Harlan and W. Crew Anderson. Copyright 1988. Harlan Anderson Press.

the hunter for cleaning and tuning. I suspect that this is an economic move on the part of the manufacturers for a couple of reasons. One is to make them cheaper to build. The other reason, I suspect, is to encourage the owner to discard it if it no longer works right, and purchase a new one. If a call can be taken apart for cleaning and tuning, it will likely outlast its owner.

IDENTIFICATION AND EVALUATION OF CALLS

VALUE OF CALLS

You will find that I have made no attempt to place a monetary value on any of the game calls in this section. To do so at this time is impossible in all but a few rare instances. There has just not been sufficient time to pass between now and the very short time ago that calls began to be recognized as a very desirable collectible. There is still a relatively small nucleus of serious collectors, but interest is growing rapidly. Until the avocation has sufficient history of sales and trade to develop a realistic secondary market the collector is encouraged to cultivate a knowledge and appreciation of calls. Their history, construction and use are, of course, fundamental to appreciating them, but the beauty and rarity of the fine call is the primary motivation for collecting them. The quality of the sound one is able to produce on the call is of secondary importance to collecting. One must give it some emphasis for after all that is the reason for their existence in the first place. What I am saying is that the quality of sound can be de-emphasized because the advances in call-making over their history has improved to such a degree as to make many of the old calls pale in comparison. One could argue further that few, if any, makers would go to the trouble of fashioning a call that would nowadays be considered collectible, if he couldn't produce the requisite sounds with it.

Once you have seen and handled a number of the finer collectible calls you will begin to be able to recognize what is good and what isn't. There is no substitute for experience. You can read this book and study the photographs and it will give you a good basis on which to build, but "hands-on" is the byword here. There are a number of things that influence the value and collectibility of a call. Here are a few of them:

MAKER—This is the most important factor in the valuation of calls. Is he a well-known maker? Was he a recognized and accomplished decoy carver?

CONDITION—Collectors differ on the importance of this factor, but all agree that the call needs to be in decent condition. As with any collectible a very rare example is desirable in just about any recognizable condition. Where condition would affect value in this instance is if you were to be contemplating purchasing and you have the opportunity of obtaining two, one of which is in good condition and the other poor. Finish and appearance would weigh heavily here, if it is to be considered at all.

PATENT MODEL—This is the extremely rare instance where you come across a call that is exactly like the drawing in the original patent application in every detail.

SPECIAL OWNER—You might encounter a relatively common call that was owned by a famous individual or used to win a world championship calling contest or to bag a world record. Whatever the circumstances, a thing called "provenance" comes into very important play. Provenance is a provable record of origin and ownership; a written, provable record of an unbroken chain of ownership from the time of the incident of famous person ownership.

QUALITY OF THE CALL, AGE, UNIQUENESS, BEAUTY AND RARITY—All of these factors are self-explanatory.

IDENTIFICATION OF CALLS

In the pages following are descriptions and photographs of some of the products of the more well-known call-makers from the various regions discussed on the previous pages. Please take note that the makers are grouped as to the *type* of call made without regard to where the maker lived or worked. Example: J.T. Beackhart of Swiftwater, Arkansas made **Reelfoot Lake Style** calls, not **Arkansas Style** calls as you might think.

CONSTRUCTION AND NOMENCLATURE OF CALLS

Most of you who are interested in collecting calls are already intimately familiar with the construction details of at least the calls you have used over the years. There will be, however, a few of you who have never used a call, so never owned one to clean and maintain and a few others who have never hunted at all. The latter are interested only from the uniqueness, beauty and collectibility of this fine example of American folk art. So, a few notes and diagrams regarding construction details and nomenclature follow.

Names of the parts have changed over the years and differ from region to region as well. This can be very confusing.

EXAMPLES:

      Stem = Stopper = Plug = Keg = Bill

      Insert = Bill = Sounding Board = Tone Board

      Reed = Tongue

      Wedge = Wedge block = Stopper

Because hunters and collectors almost universally use "Stopper" and "Insert" interchangeably, they will be used so in this work.

In the interest of alleviating any confusion due to the above examples it is best to standardize the names of these parts in this book. The following diagrams of the four major types of calls should help you avoid any further confusion.

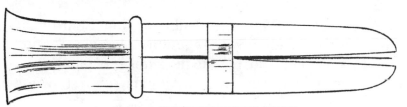

Figure 1. TONGUE PINCHER STYLE

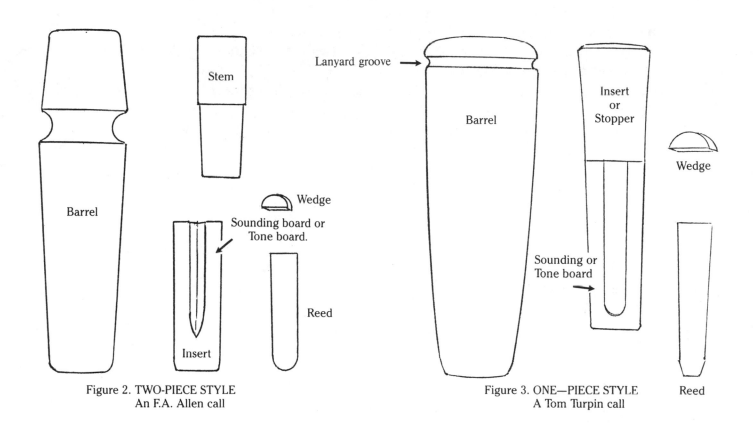

Stem

Lanyard groove →

Barrel

Insert or Stopper

Wedge

Barrel

Wedge

Sounding board or Tone board.

Insert

Reed

Sounding or Tone board

Figure 2. TWO-PIECE STYLE
An F.A. Allen call

Figure 3. ONE—PIECE STYLE
A Tom Turpin call

Reed

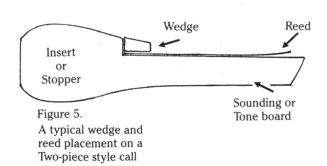

Wedge   Reed

Insert or Stopper

Figure 5.
A typical wedge and reed placement on a Two-piece style call

Sounding or Tone board

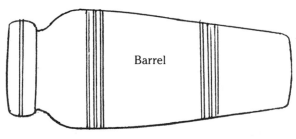

Barrel

Figure 4.   BARREL AND INSERT with Wedge and reed, typical Arkansas call
A Chick Major call

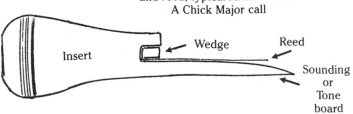

Insert   Wedge   Reed

Sounding or Tone board

Some clarification of the Insert (Stopper)/Stem/Sounding or Tone Board relationship is necessary to understanding their location and construction with regard to "One-piece" and "Two-piece" styles.

The "One" and "Two" in the style names do not refer to the number of parts in a call but rather to whether the Insert (Stopper) is made of one or two pieces. Figure 3 and Figure 5 show the parts of a typical One-piece style and how they go together. Note that the Insert is made in one piece. Now take a look at Figure 2. Note that the insert consists only of the Tone Board. In order to assemble the call, the Reed must be placed on the Tone Board, the Wedge on the Reed, then pushed into the part named the Stem. This assembly is then inserted into the Barrel to complete the call. The Stem in this particular instance is made of metal, but it could be made of any other material.

These diagrams also serve to illustrate the differences between the Rounded or Curved Radius Sounding or Tone Boards and between the straight and curved reed.

Materials for call bodies typically used over the years have been Bakelite, plastics, hard rubber, all sorts of woods and metal. Wedges have been made of cork or some other wood mostly and reed are plastic, metal or hard rubber. Sometime the use of particular materials in a call are somewhat like a maker's signature. It can be a great help in identifying a call in some instances; in others, useless. When significant these characteristics will be covered in individual listings.

BOOKS AND PUBLICATIONS ABOUT CALLS

There have been only three books about collecting duck and other game calls published so far and I personally know of only one being worked on now and it has no scheduled publication date as yet. That, plus a rare few magazine articles in the **Ducks Unlimited** magazine and **American Shotgunner** is the complete body of work about collecting duck calls. There are, of course, other publications at least partially devoted to calls, but they are, for the most part, about using calls.

There are also two associations of call makers and collectors. The addresses are listed following books and other publications.

BOOKS

DUCK CALLS AND OTHER GAME CALLS by Brian J. McGrath. Copyright 1988. The Thomas B. Reel Company, 2005 Tree House, Plano, TX 75023. Hardbound, 8″ × 10½″, 150 pages. A very good guide to collecting calls. Well illustrated with descriptive entries of makers and the characteristics and styles of their products. This book was issued in a limited edition of 950 and my copy, purchased in early 1991, is numbered 947. There may be some available, but you will have to contact the publisher.

DUCK CALLS, AN ENDURING AMERICAN FOLK ART by Howard L. Harlan and W. Crew Anderson. Copyright 1988. Harlan Anderson Press, 4920 Franklin Road, Nashville, TN 37220. Hardbound, 8½″ × 11″, 316 pages. An exhaustive and scholarly study of the American duck call and its history. This large limited edition book is a must for anyone interested in collecting duck calls. Harlan and Anderson obviously devoted considerable time to the research, photography and writing of this very fine book.

REELFOOT LAKE, HISTORY-DUCK CALL MAKERS-HUNTING TALES, Revised Edition by Russell H. Caldwell. Copyright 1989. Calwell's Office Outfitters, Inc., Union City, TN 38261. Hardbound, 5½″ × 8½″. 272 pages. Anyone interested in Reelfoot Lake Style duck calls could not possibly do without this book. Written by a native and lifetime resident of the area, hunter and sportsman Caldwell has compiled what has to be the definitive work on the history and identification of duck calls and their makers of the Reelfoot Lake area.

DUCKS, HOW TO CALL THEM by Tom Turpin. Copyright date unknown. This is an old 50 page softbound, 5½″ × 8½″ booklet that is interesting and chock full of calling advice. What makes it useful is Turpin's drawing anbd specs for his calls. I have only a photocopy and know of no source for these.

DUCK CALLING by Earl Dennison. Copyright date unknown. This is another old 5″ × 7½″, softbound 60 page booklet. Anyone interested in the history of duck calls should try to obtain a copy. I got mine from W.F. "Tom" Dennison, Earl's son, who runs Dennison Sporting Goods, Box 116, Hwy 51 South, Newbern, TN. He may have some more copies.

PERIODICALS

THE DECOY HUNTER, 901 North 9th Street, Clinton, Indiana 47842. This is a bi-monthly magazine devoted to collecting decoys that has occasional articles and advertising for duck calls. Worth subscribing to because with growing interest will probably come more articles.

SPORTING CLASSICS, P.O. Box 1017, Hwy 521 South, Camden, South Carolina 29020. A slick monthly magazine about any and all sporting collectibles. The same comments applied to the DECOY HUNTER above apply here.

ORGANIZATIONS

CALLMAKERS AND COLLECTORS ASSOCIATION OF AMERICA, 303 Murphreesboro Road, Nashville, Tennessee 37210. This is a national organization presently with over 200 members and growing. They publish a very nice and informative newsletter. Any collector or potential collector will find membership indispensable.

REELFOOT LAKE CALL MAKERS AND COLLECTORS ASSOCIATION, P.O. Box 748, Union City, Tennessee 38261. This is a new organization for, as the name implies, those specializing in Reelfoot Lake Style calls. It is in its infancy now, but promises exciting things in the future for collectors.

A HISTORY OF DUCK AND GAME CALLS

Until just a few years ago there was precious little written material with regard to the origins and early history of the development of bird calls in America. What little we have now is, however, a valuable asset to the collecting of these calls. The writers creating those works are to be commended for the valuable contributions they have so far made, and encouraged to continue research as they have indicated they intend to do. Two of the three books so far written have attempted to divide the historical evolution of calls into stages. Interestingly, although working independently, those authors came up with essentially in the same divisions. *McGrath gives names to these divisions in his book, but **Harlan and Anderson do not in theirs. In the interest of trying to standardize these divisions for future research and writing I suggest adopting McGrath's five divisions of: "Prior History," "Early Times," "The Golden Age," "Quiet Times" and "The New Golden Age" with a couple of minor alterations in the interest of further clarification. My suggestion, proffered with due respect, is to change only the names of the first two division to "Primitive Times" and "Early History" respectively. Chronology and events would remain as already delineated.

PRIMITIVE TIMES (Pre 1850's)

This would be the time before we have any concrete, demonstrable evidence of a man-made object, fashioned expressly for the luring of wild game to within a killing distance by imitating the calls or sounds. At some point in time in early North America some pre-historic being likely may have successfully mimicked the cry of a wild animal with his own vocal cords and mouth in order to lure it in. It is also likely that earl on, primitive man would develop the talent for using whatever might be at hand for imitating game sounds. Certainly the American Indians developed this to a high degree. They are known to have, and still do for that matter, used whistles and reeds (Have you ever placed a blade of grass between your thumbs and blown a shrill call?). Certainly any peoples capable of creating the beautiful decoys found in the Lovelock Cave excavations in Nevada (see page 3) were sophisticated enough to have fashioned some sort of calling device. The problem is that there has not yet been anything like that uncovered in any North American archelogical excavation so far.

*Duck Calls and Other Game Calls by Brian J. McGrath. Copyright 1988, Thomas B. Reel, Co., Plano, TX
**Duck Calls, an Enduring American Folk Art by Howard Harlan and W. Crew Anderson. Copyright 1988, Harlan Anderson Press, Nashville, TN.

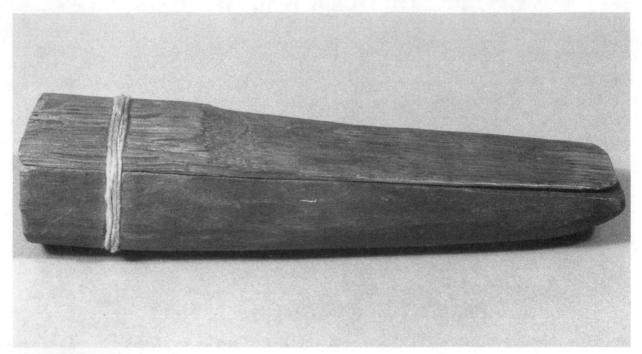

This is a very primitive call from the Reelfoot Lake area of Tennessee. It measures 4¾", has a wooden reed and is very difficult to blow. A unique duck call that very likely represents earliest attempts at making calls.

EARLY HISTORY (1850's-1935)

The areas of most concentrated activity in this period of the development of commerical call making are the Illinois River and the Reelfoot Lake area in Tennessee. There are distinct differences in the style of call from each of these regions, but that will be covered later.

So far collectors and writers have only been able to trace "production" calls back to 1854 or slightly before. Harlan and Anderson made the observation that there appears to be a "Tongue Pincher" style of duck call clipped or otherwise attached to the left breast pocket of a hunter's coat in a Currier and Ives print dated 1854. If you are curious to see the print there is a detail of it reproduced in their book or, if you wish to view the real print in it's entirety you may find one archived or on display in a nearby gallery or museum. The print is entitled WILD DUCK SHOOTING/A GOOD DAYS SPORT. It is a stone lithograph of a painting by Arthur Fitzwilliam Tait (1819-1905). Certainly that is evidence that they were being produced prior to 1854. It could, however, be an English call brought over by settlers or visitors. Only time will tell.

The earliest real evidence of American production of a duck call is in the form of a patent issued to an Elam Fisher of Detroit in 1870 for a "Tongue Pincher" type call. More about Fisher later.

The is a scarcity of information about this period of time, but there was apparently a surge of interest and activity among call makers then, and there seems to have developed some amount of competition among them. This is evidence by the above patent and advertising claims by Fred A. Allen of Monmouth, Illinois and Charles W. Grubbs of Chicago, that each was the first to offer a production duck call commerically. Grubbs claimed he did so in 1868 in a 1928 advertisement and the authors of **Decoys and Decoy Carvers of the Illinois River**, Paul W. Parmalee and Forrest D. Loomis state in their book that "Allen's Nickel-Plated Duck Caller" was made for private use in 1863 and "...was considered to be the first duck call to be mass produced in Illinois." Whatever the case it is ample evidence of commerical call-making activity at that early date. It is important to note here that the Elam Fisher call was the first to have utilized a barrel, thus creating a resonant chamber for the call. His "Nickel Plated Duck Call" is recognized as a significant development in call making and examples of them are highly collectible.

As far as can be determined so far, it looks as if no one got the bright idea to advertise their products until the early 1880's. It seems almost absurd that it wouldn't occur to these folks for ten or fifteen years, but so far a search of old magazines and catalogs hasn't turned up any. Whatever the case, they took up advertising with a vengeance from the early 1880's on.

Here were some distinctly different styles invented and refined during the Early History period. The **Illinois Style** and the **Reelfoot or Glodo Style** were the first to be developed, followed closely by the **Arkansas Style** and concurrently, the **Louisiana or Cajun Style** utilizing bamboo or cane (as it is known in the South) instead of wood or other substances. Refer to the Construction and Nomenclature section for details regarding the differences between these different styles.

There were many variations and experiments in the development of the styles, but one that has survived through the years is that of Victor Glodo of Reelfoot Lake. All the others made contributions of varying importance, but the **Glodo** or **Reelfoot Style** is the one that survived intact. Glodo moved to Reelfoot Lake around 1890. Until recently it was thought that Glodo was a French Canadian, but we know that he came from a call-making family that hailed from the Fountain Bluff Area of southern Illinois. His calls were of the two-piece type utilizing a wooden wedge block, a flat tone board and a curved metal reed (See the Tom Turpin call illustrated in the Construction and Nomenclature section). The **Glodo** and **Reelfoot Style** of duck call is the most widely used style of metal reed design in call making today. The fact that he was the first maker to decorate his calls (he was the first to use checkering) makes him the father of the American duck calls as a folk art in the estimation of most aficionados.

This important era, the Early History Period, in the evolution of duck call making can be laid out more clearly in the following illustrated chronology:

c1854-1870

First patent of the *Tongue pincher style* duck call, characterized by a straight reed sandwiched between two rounded or curved radius tone boards bound together; no barrel. 1854 Currier and Ives lithograph possibly illustrating this type. Elam Fisher-1870, Charles Schoenhieder-1880.

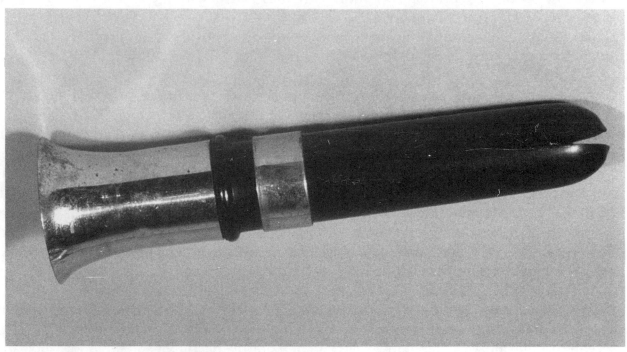

From the Howard Harlan collection

An Elam Fisher Tongue Pincher Style duck call measuring 4¾". Either an Elam Fisher or Red Duck product. Note the shiny metal trumpet typical of this type call.

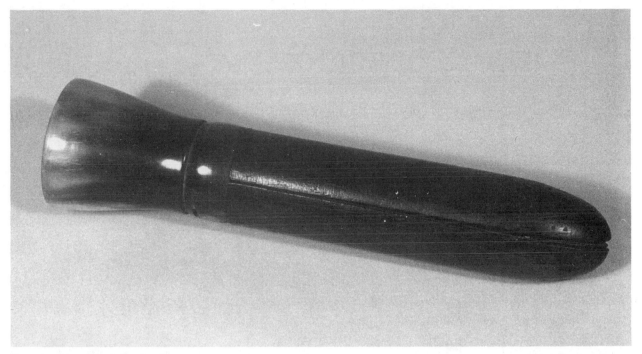

From the Howard Harlan collection

This 5½″ wood and horn Tongue Pincher Style duck call is an Elam Fisher design, but not substantiated as one of his. Could be a Red Duck product. Some very similar to this have been found with "ELAM FISHER, DETROIT, MICH" stamped on them.

c1863-1870

Early Illinois River Style. Characterisized by a curved metal reed, a single straight or flat tone board (two-piece stem and insert) a half-round cork wedge block and a barrel. First known use of the barrel to create a resonant chamber is attributed to Fred A. Allen. Others making this style call were Charles W. Grubbs of Chicago, who claimed he was making them as early as 1868 and advertised his calls at least as early as 1892 and George Peterson, who was in business in 1873 making decoys and perhaps duck calls as early as that also. The Peterson business was bought out by Jasper N. Dodge ten years later about 1883. The **Early Illinois River Style** continued to be made into the 1900's even though the variation known as the **Later Illinois River Style** had been developed on was being utilized in call making, also in the 1900's. The **Later Illinois River Style**, however, is more appropriately discussed in the next period of this chronology.

The **Reelfoot** or **Glodo Style** was originated by Victor Glodo of Reelfoot lake. It is characterized by the use of a curved metal reed held to a straight, one-piece (combination stem and insert) tone board by a wooden wedge block inserted into a barrel. Glodo was the first to decorate duck calls. He used checkering.

These are three sizes of Fred A. Allen metal duck calls. They measure 3⅞″, 4⅛″ and 5″ respectively. These were developed in the 1860-70's.

Another design by Fred A. Allen. the length of this fairly big call is 6½″ overall. Stamped on the metal stem is "F.A. ALLEN MONMOUTH, ILL."

From the Howard Harlan collection

A 6⅛″ Charles W. Grubbs duck call. May be a fairly early example of his production calls.

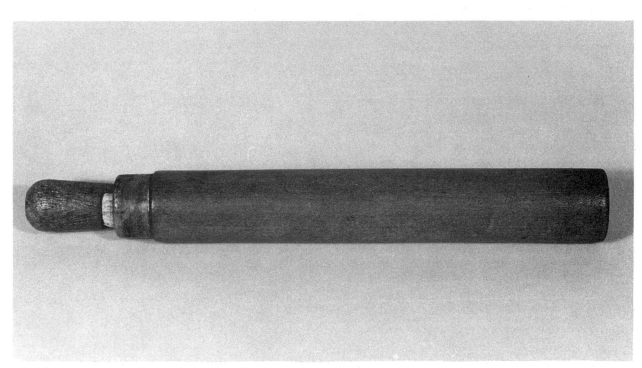

From the Howard Harlan collection

This very long, 8¼″ call may be one of the very first calls made by Grubbs. It is an **Early Illinois River Style** call with a cork wedge block, metal reed and flat tone board.

This fine looking call represents Grubbs' final top of his line production model Called the "Perfection Duck Call," this 6½″ call was available as late as the 1920's. Interestingly most of his calls made after the initial Illinois Rivers styles were of the **Reelfoot** or **Glodo Style**.

This 5¼″ call is the last known style of a Grubbs production duck call.

The unusual looking screw eye type device on the barrel of this Grubbs call is known as the "FULLER DEVICE." In 1903 a David S. Fuller of Chicago was granted a patent for a device that could adjust the tone of a duck call. This is the only example of a call with the Fuller Device installed known to exist.

When Victor Glodo died in 1910, the tradition and form of the style he originated was carried on by Tom Turpin and after Turpin's death, the late J.L. Melancon of Robeline, Louisiana bought the business from this estate. With regard to this particular Glodo call Turpin told Melancon that it was the first call Glodo made. It is completely hand-carved, asymmetrical in shape and bears rather crude checkering.

This 5½″ Glodo is a good example of where his calls in the final years of production.

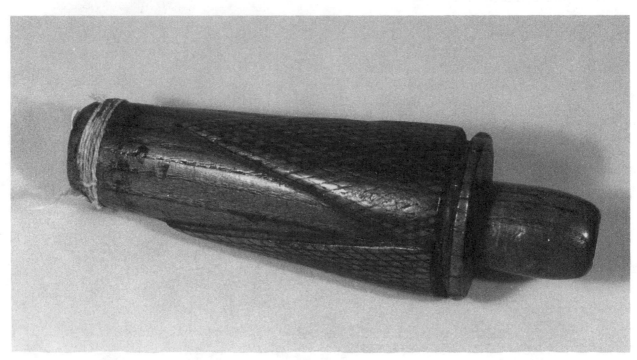

John Nickolas Glodo of Victor Glodo's family in the Fountain Bluff area of southern Illinois fashioned this 5¼″ duck call. It is essentially the same form and design of the Victor Glodo calls with the exception of the flat top of the barrel.

1880's-1910's

The **Tongue Pincher Style** continued to be made into the 1910's by Fisher and Schoenhieder. Others who joined them in the making of them were the Bridgeport Gun and Implement, Co. (B.G.I.) in Connecticut, a company named Red Duck Calls and the N.C. Hansen Company of Zimmerman, Minnesota. All made their calls in the Elam Fisher design. The Hansen Company was still advertising these calls (albeit modified) In the late 1940's, **Early Illinois River Style** calls continued to be made into this period by Charles H. Ditto of Keithsburg, Illinois (he made other styles also) and James W. Reynolds, Chicago, who became more known for his "Double Duck Call" patented in 1906. Charles H. Perdew of Henry, Illinois also produced calls in the **Early Illinois River Style**.

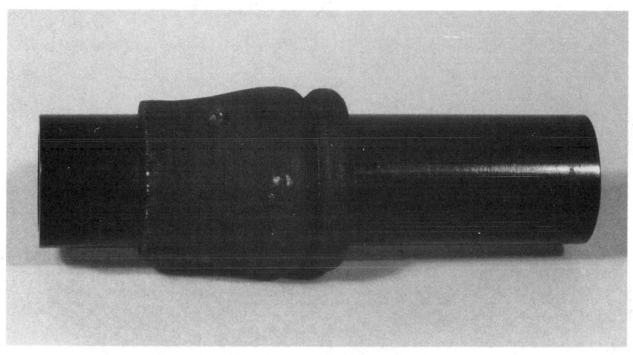

From the Howard Harlan collection

The 4½″ Reynolds "DOUBLE DUCK" call.

This 5½″ call is attributed to Charles H. Perdew of Henry, Illinois. His calls are of the **Early Illinois River Style**. Take note of the crown design stopper or insert. Though he carved other birds on his calls this is the only known instance of a teal. Visible at left, on the bottom of the barrel is a rim of colored plastic. Collectors call this "Candy." In this instance it is green. Candy also occurs in red and amber with amber being the earliest. Extremely rare.

Pictured here is a very nice 6¼″ Perdew call with amber colored "Candy." This one depicts a mallard drake and hen. It is imprinted with the initials "PWM."

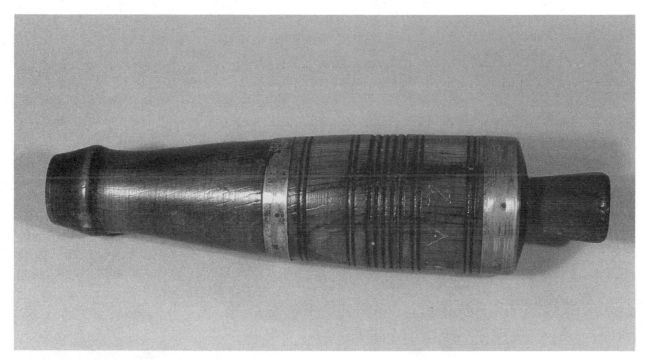

This very large Perdew call is the biggest and rarest of his duck calls. It measures 7⅛″ long and 1¾″ in diameter.

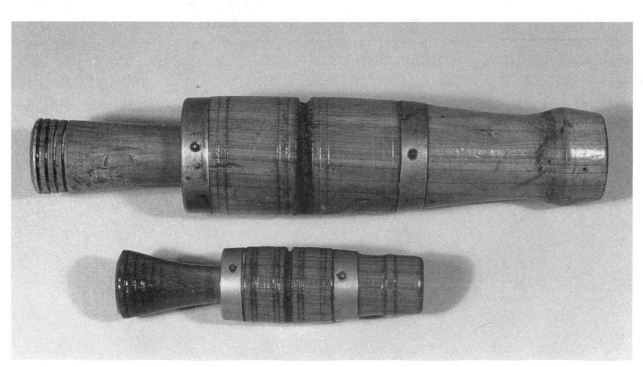

Upper call in this photo is a standard Perdew call measuring 5⅝″ overall. The miniature is only 3″ long. It is thought that he made only a couple dozen of these unique little calls.

This is an example of a 6″ call Perdew for Von Lengerke and Antoine (VL&A), a sporting goods company, to market with their imprint. If you look closely you can make out the "VL&A" on the panel along the barrel.

The **Later Illinois River Style** was developed during this period (c1903). This is the era when the hard rubber call and reed were developed. August L. Kuhlemeier of Burlington, Iowa was the first to patent this, but may not have necessarily been the inventor. For some unknown reason the **Later Illinois River Style** was characterized by a return to the older rounded radius or curved tone board and straight reed (both of hard rubber frequently). They also utilize cork wedge blocks. The call that represents this style as developed to a high art was that made by Philip Sanford Olt. His company, P.S. Olt, Pekin, Illinois, developed a call they dubbed the "D-2" that, with some minor changes, has been successfully made and sold since 1904. The company is still in business today.

A D-2 call made by the P.S. Olt Company. the imprint you see on the barrel is repeated on the insert in smaller letters.

A P.S. Olt D-2 duck call broken down into its components.

Reelfoot or **Glodo Style** duck calls. Victor Glodo died in 1910, but the style he developed was continued by Tom Turpin of Memphis, Tennessee; J.T. Beckhart, Swiftwater, Arkansas; John "Sundown" Cochran, Samburg, Tennessee, whose son John "Son" Cochran continues to make calls in this classic style and form today; and G.D. Kinney of Hughes, Tennessee.

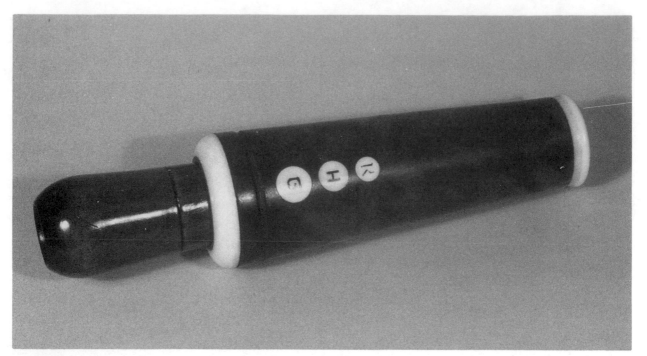

This is a very handsome Turpin call made especially for a member of the famous B.F. Goodrich family. Take note of the ivory touches on the ends and the initials "RHG" in the circular ivory inlays.

Another fine custom made Tom Turpin call. This one measures 6¾″ and is rendered in top line burled walnut.

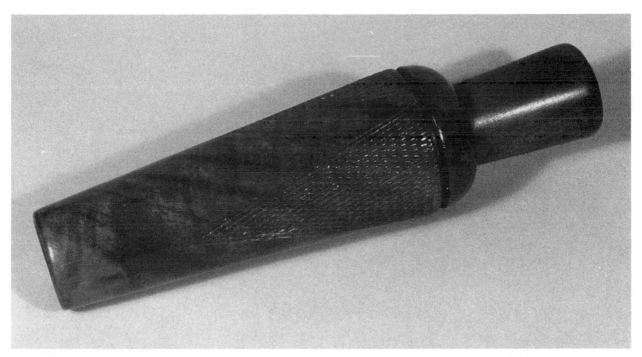

An excellent example of Tom Turpin's work. This is a direct copy of a Victor Glodo. It is not easy to see in this photo, but the call bears very fine checkering.

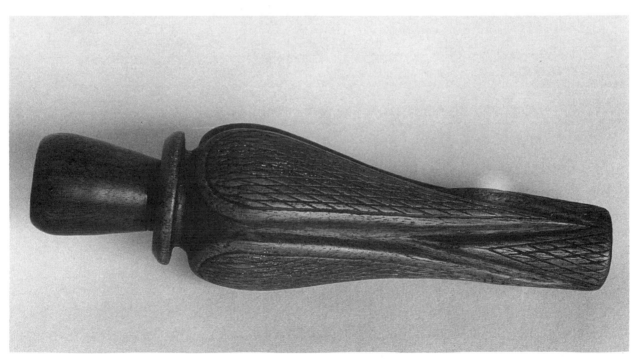

Reelfoot Lake Style maker J.T. Beckhart made this good looking call. Smooth lines and beautiful workmanship are typical of Beckhart calls.

From the Howard Harlan collection

Another J.T. Beckhart duck call. 5¾". Note the silver rim around the bottom or lip of the call.

From the Howard Harlan collection

A 5¾ inch call made by John E. "Sundown" Cochran of Hornbeak, Tennessee. He was a student of Glodo and his calls are much like Glodo's. They are easily identified as he habitually stamped them "MADE BY J.E. COCHRAN HORNBEAK TENN." Sometimes he would add "REELFOOT LAKE" and some would be stamped with his price of "$5.00." Only a handful have been found without some sort of stamped identification.

This call was made by John Cochran, son of "Sundown" Cochran. He carries on the tradition by continuing to fashion calls in the type and form his father used. The checkering and other decoration on the barrel was done by a local Reelfoot Lake artisan.

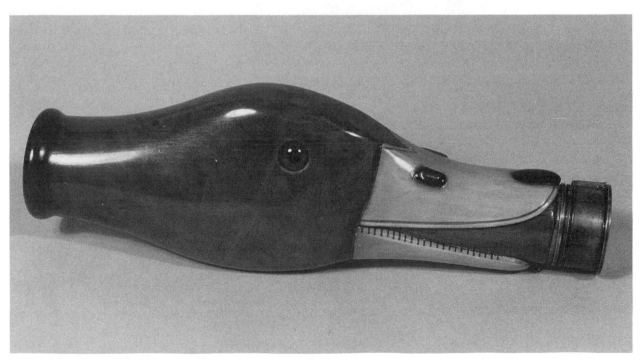

This beautifully rendered duck call is the product of the combined effort of C.L.V. Kinney and William F. Harlow of Newark, Ohio. They were co-workers in the same company and good friends who made duck calls together. This one is made of ivory and bodock (also known as mock orange or osage orange) with some brass for the shell in the duck's mouth. It also has glass eyes and measures 6¼″ long. Interesting this particular call utilizes the Elam Fisher **Tongue Pincher Style** reed and tone board. See next photo.

If we assume the previous Kinney and Harlow to be a prototype, then this slightly smaller version is the production call. It looks the same, but therein the similarlity ends. It is entirely leather covered except for the brass portion of the shell. Stamped into the end of the brass shell are the words: "Kinney and Harlow Newark Ohio." It also has a glass eye but is a bit shorter at 6″. The most important difference is that the sound mechanism of these is of the **Reelfoot Lake Style**, which places it in this section.

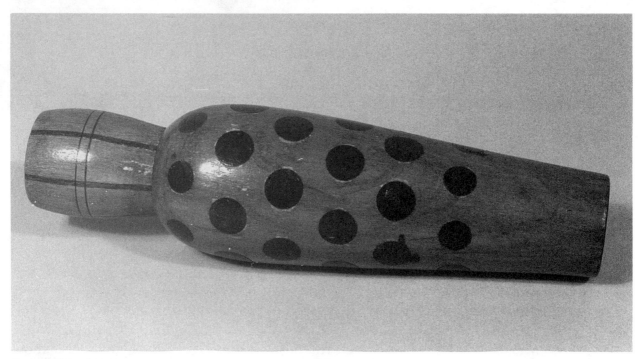

This fine looking **Reelfoot Lake Style** call was made by William F. Harlow of Kinney and Harlow. Note the very nice inlay work on the barrel and insert.

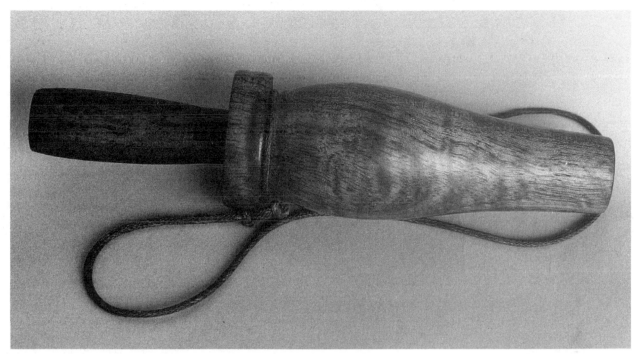

John Edward Jolly of Memphis was a **Reelfoot Lake Style** maker. He began making calls in the 1920's while living in Arkansas. He moved to Memphis in the 1930's. This plain barrel call was made while he still lived in Arkansas.

The upper, 6⅞″ call in this photo probably represents a transition from plain to decorated calls. He began checkering and getting more elaborate and making fewer and fewer calls as the years went by. His carved and decorated calls exhibit a heavy J.T. Beckhart influence. The little 3⅝″ miniature in the photo is the only one presently known to exist.

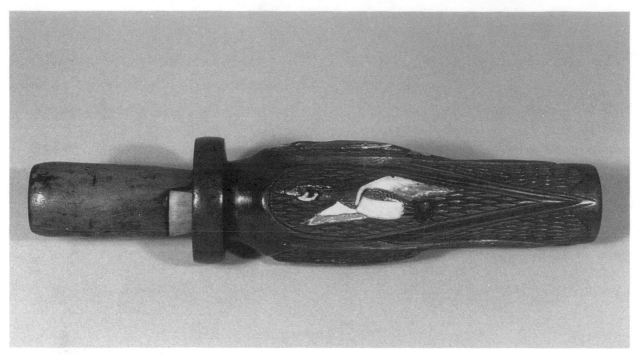

Although it is estimated that Jolly fashioned around a thousand of his plain barrel calls, he only produced about one hundred of the carved and decorated calls. As in this photo he would carve and paint ducks of various species on the carved panels of the barrel. One of the panels would frequently bear the owner's initials, name or a symbol such as the Masonic emblem.

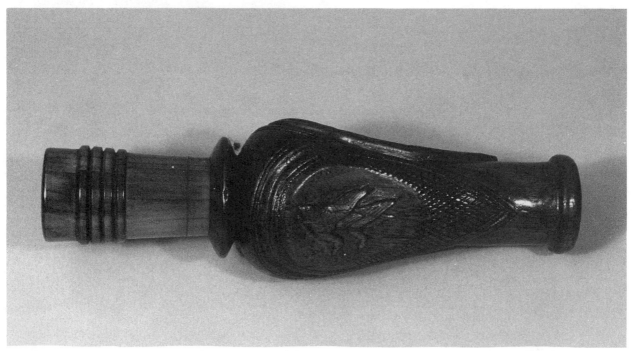

William Burke, Memphis, was another **Reelfoot Lake Style** maker. He was never a commerical call maker, but rather fashioned them for friends therefore they are rare. The 5½″ example here is one of the most elaborate. His others all adhere to the same shape or form but vary from plain barrel to grooved to checkered.

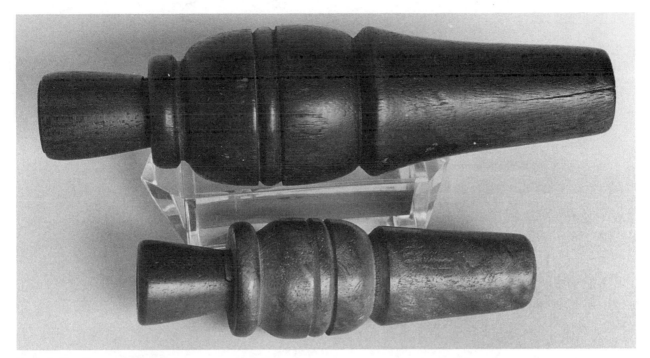

From the Tom Barre collection

These **Reelfoot Lake Style** calls were made by Henry Kenward and/or the Kenward family. Two other names associated with the family, from the Jonesboro, Arkansas area, are John Kenward and Sydney Kenward. Made in the 1920's and 1930's these are called the New Beckhart calls because "THE NEW BECKHART ***" is found stamped on the flat end of the barrel where the insert is. The smaller miniature call does not bear the imprint. These calls are rare and desirable, but are in no way connected to the J.T. Beckhart calls discussed on previous pages so be careful not to confuse them.

Another **Reelfoot Lake Style** duck call. This one is a product of R. Kelso of Alenandria, Louisiana. This very fine call shows a decidedly strong influence on Kelso's work by J.T. Beckhart. Note the use of horn on both ends of the barrel. You may be able to make out the stamped imprint "R KELSO" at the left end of the barrel.

Perry Hooker of Memphis was another maker of calls in the **Reelfoot Lake Style**. This long, 7¾″ Hooker is decorated with a number of painted mallards that are a bit worn.

Form the Howard Harlan collection

This Hooker calls is interesting in that he carved ducks onto four sides using as his pattern, four scenes printed on the sides of 1930's vintage Remington shell boxes. It measures 6¼″ long.

From the Howard Harlan collection

Another view of the same Hooker call. Hooker sold his and call making equipment in the 1940's to three gentlemen and taught them his methods. The new calls were called and labeled "BENJON MEMPHIS" rather stylistically with the Memphis smaller and beneath the Benjon. Apparently some stock with the sale as some Hooker made some calls for the new owners for some have been found with "HOOKER DUCK CALL" stamped on the end of the insert or stopper.

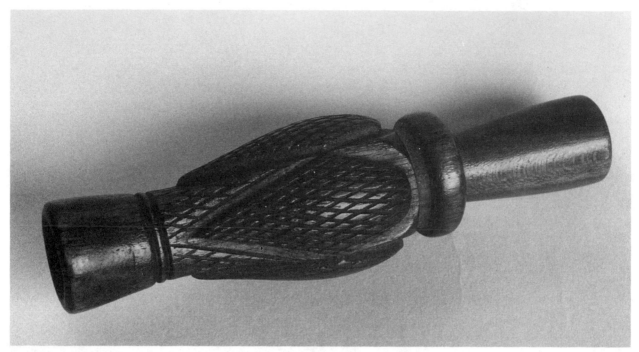

This call in the **Reelfoot Lake Style**, was made by O.K. "Pop" Pickle of Otwell, Arkansas. He was likely working in the 1910's and 1920's. His son Leonard made calls also, in the same style and form as his father. As you can see from the photo Pickle was truly aware of the aesthetic qualities of a finely crafted duck call. Calls from both father and son are highly desirable.

Claude C. Stone was another maker of **Reelfoot Lake Style** duck calls. Stone is another maker heavily influenced by the Beckhart form, but his calls have a distinct look and beauty of their own. An almost universal trademark of Stone was his carving of a stylized "S" into checkering or decoration on the barrels of his calls.

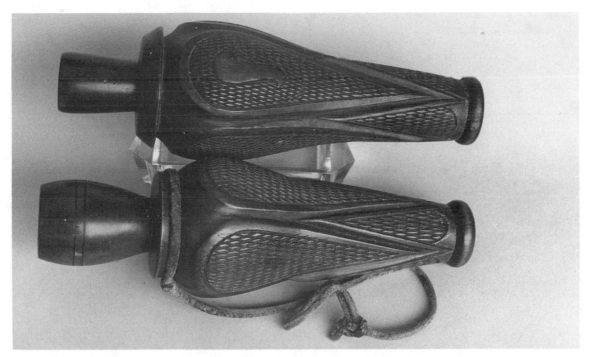

From the Tom Barre collection

This photo is of two more Stone duck calls. The upper call in the photograph has the wrong stopper in it. The stopper is, in fact, a "Pop" Pickle stopper. The latter is an illustration of something you may run into from time to time in your collecting activities.

From the Howard Harlan collection

Yet another maker influenced by Beckhart is Jo Willingham who made calls in the early 1900's. Although not always, Willingham would often stamp his calls with the words: "JO MADE IT." This particular call is marked with "JO. WILLINGHAM PINE BLUFF ARK" cast into a flat silver ring placed around the flat top of the call where the stopper is inserted. This one-of-a-kind call was his personal call.

217

Ezra Cochran made **Reelfoot Lake Style** duck calls around the 1930's and 1940's. He was from Pine Bluff, Arkansas and was taught by Jo Willingham. His form remains essentially the same, but they are found with and without checkering and carving as in this 4¾″ long example. These are highly prized calls.

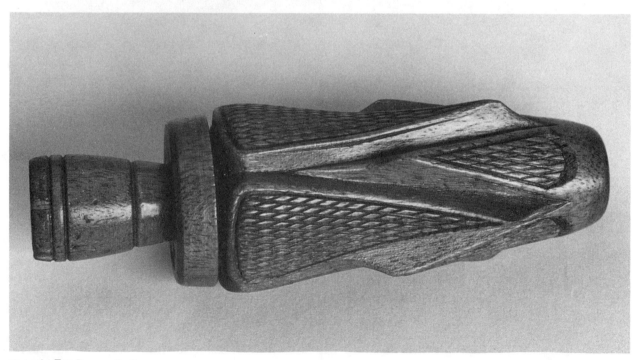

A very fine example of a W.E. "Buck" Boyd duck call. It is easily identifiable by his stamping quite plainly on the flat end of the barrel where the stopper is inserted: "W.E. BOYD."

c1920-1935

All of the styles covered so far continued to be produced in various numbers, from few to many, all through this period of time, but there were two more styles that developed almost concurrently. Each is a variation of the preceding style, but with sufficient differences to render them unique.

The **Arkansas Style** is thought to be a modified version of the **Illinois River Style** and it is quite obvious that the P.S. Olt calls have a strong influence on the construction of the **Arkansas Style** calls. The calls are constructed of wood for the most part, and the one-piece stem has a notch cut out at the beginning of the tone board so that the straight reed could be held in independent of insertion of the stem into the barrel (see page 186). It is likely that the **Arkansas Style** evolved around the late 1910's. Presently it appears that the earliest makers are probably Clyde Hancock and W.T. Lancaster, both of Stuttgart, Arkansas, followed closely by *A.M. Bowles of Little Rock in the mid 1920's and Darce Manning "Chick" Major of Stuttgart on the early 1930's.

From the Howard Harlan collection

This **Arkansas Style** 5⅛" duck call is attributed to Clyde Hancock of Stuttgart, Arkansas. It does not bear his usual square red and gold label with his name and town on it, but it may have been worn off with use, cleaning and handling over the years. Otherwise it looks like a Hancock.

* It has been reported that Bowles took up the making of duck calls when his son quit making them in 1935. There is also an advertisement in a 1938 issue of *Outdoor Life* that states in its headline: "Hand Carved Duck Calls Since 1927." A statement further on in the ad: y 20 years of making Big Lake Duck Calls..." confuses the issue. If you use simple math and accept the advertising copy claim you come out with 1907, but if you use the publishing date of the magazine you get 1918.

A.M. "Andy" Bowles made calls in four distinct designs, all in the **Arkansas Style**. The checkered example pictured here is the considered the most desirable by collectors. The earliest style calls are unmarked but are plain barrel, slightly tapered toward the blowing end and with a slight carved "waist." The next style, also plain barrel, looks somewhat like the last 6″ to 8″ of a baseball bat handle with the knob cut flat on the edges. The latter and other, later Bowles calls found will generally be marked "A.M. BOWLES LITTLE ROCK, ARK." around the top where the stem is inserted.

A nice Chick Major call measuring 5⅛″ long. This one can be dated to the 1950's by the red and gold decal with the notched corners. Major started making calls in the 1930's and continued to make them until his death in 1974. His earliest calls had no label or decal, he simply signed them. The next, his c1940's calls, were stamped simply, "DIXIE."

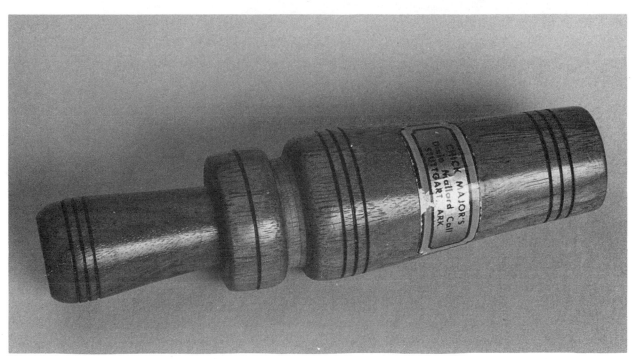

Another **Arkansas Style** 1950's call made by Chick Major in a slightly different barrel design.

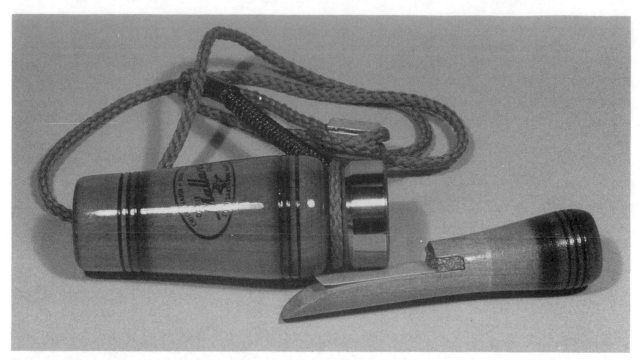

A handsome 1960's-1970's Chick Major call (the clear and black label is of that time) broken down partially to illustrate the classic **Arkansas Style** manner of constructing the reed retention on the insert. Note the similarity with the P.S. Olts call discussed and illustrated on previous pages.

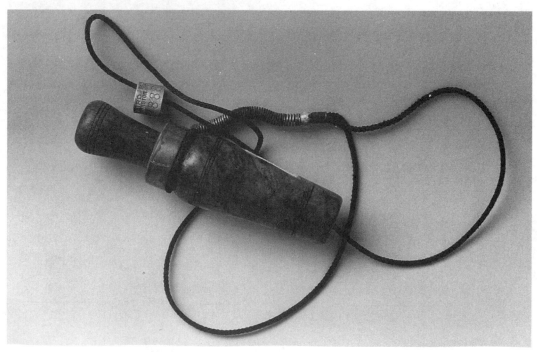

From the Tom Barre collection

This Chick Major call was found in the Black River Refuge in Arkansas by a game warden in 1985. It is in remarkable shape and still blows pretty good.

From the Tom Barre collection

An excellent example of an **Arkansas Style** duck call made by Jake Gartner. This one is lettered by hand in gold paint on the barrel as follows: "Jake Gartner R U.S. PAT. OFF. 53716 WORLD'S CHAMPION 1947-48-49." Gartner's and Major's early call were similar, so be careful not to confuse them.

It may be difficult to believe, but these two **Arkansas Style** duck calls were made by the same man. Mark Weedman, Little Rock, started making beautiful wooden calls in the 1930's. The upper call is a nice example. These early calls are the most desirable to collectors, but some of the later plastic (acrylic) models are collectible also. He started making the latter in the 1950's and as far as is known, no longer fashions calls from wood. The black and white photo does no justice to the acrylic call. There are red, white, blue, orange, silver, yellow and amber colored laminations making up this call. It and his other acrylic calls are identified by the words: "WEEDY'S PIN OAK" found stamped around the top where the stem is inserted.

Louisiana Style or **Cajun Style** duck calls as they are sometimes called, have probably been around as long as the **Arkansas Style** calls, but for now we cannot substantiate any commerical production before the 1930's. The earliest names associated with the **Louisiana Style** calls are Faulk and Airhart. Clarence "Patin" Faulk of Lake Charles is known to have made calls much earlier than the 1935 date generally accepted as when he began making calls to be sold in commerical quantities. Although he produced thousands of calls, it wasn't until 1950, when his son Dudley Faulk went into business, that we recognized the company as it exists doing business today, Faulk Calls. The other famous name in the **Louisiana Style** of call making is Allen J. Airhart. He started the Cajun Call Company in Lake Charles in 1944. It is still in business today. Although many are made of wood and other materials today, most classic **Louisiana Style** calls are made of cane. They are generally of the two-piece design much like the F.A. Allen calls described and illustrated on previous pages.

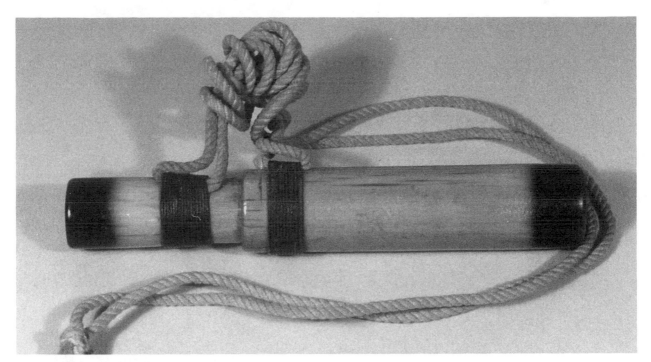

From the Howard Harlan collection

A classic 4¾″ **Louisiana/Cajun Style** duck call made of cane (bamboo to you folks from outside the South).

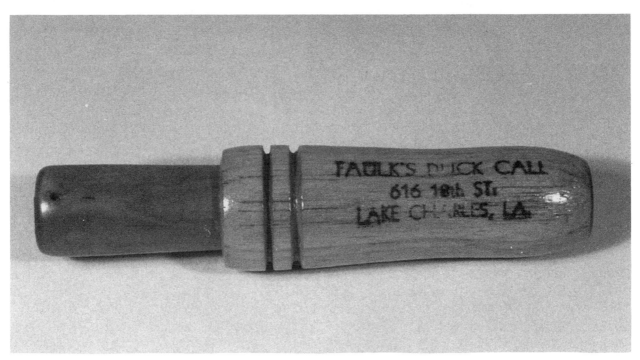

From the Howard Harlan collection

A nice Faulk's Duck Call measuring 4⅛″.

Another very nice **Louisiana/Cajun Style** call by an unknown maker. Note the use of about a 28 gauge Remington shell casing.

THE GOLDEN AGE 1935-1950

The EARLY HISTORY ERA was a terrific growth and development era in call making where everyone was experimenting and perfecting what they thought were the best in effective game calls, but there really wasn't an impetus for large scale manufacturing until 1935. Heretofore using baited field and/or live decoys wasn't uncommon, especially in the Mississippi Flyway. Who needed to produce calls in any quantities when you have the benefit of having a few live English calling ducks or "Suzys" as they were affectionately known. One could actually have the double benefit of live ducks making real live, authentic calls when desired and a few family pets at the same time. In 1935 two significant things happened that would have a profound and lasting effect on the way wildfowlers pursued their prey. First, Ducks Unlimited was formed in the interest of proper wildlife management and conservation and the second, the federal government made baiting fields and the use of live decoys illegal.

Now—there was suddenly a very good reason for obtaining and learning to use game calls. Thus was born the GOLDEN YEARS era on duck call making. Many of the older call making operations expanded to accommodate this sudden increase in demand. They began producing thousands of call even as new companies were born also producing calls in the thousands to meet this demand. Everybody and his brother seemed to be in the call making business. Some of the big names were the P.S. Olt Company turning out several thousand calls a year, decoy makers got into the business, big sporting goods firms such as Von Lengerke and Antoine (VL&A) of Chicago, Sears Roebuck, H.D. Folsom Arms Company and the like, began commissioning call makers to manufacture calls for sale through their stores and catalogs, some even with their own logos on them. It was an exciting time with abundant game and calls to attract it. This was also the time when duck calling competition came into its own.

QUIET TIMES (c1950-1970's)

About 1950 the wildfowl population had dwindled. Good efforts were being made at conservation, but it was slow to get started and gain support. It came almost too late. At this point in time general interest in hunting wildfowl was on the wane and the number of hunters was declining. There were a good many commerical call making companies out there doing business at the time. The decline of wildfowl population and hunter interest and the ready availability of inexpensive, manufactured duck calls combined, put quite a damper on the business of hand-production of fine duck call. This depressed situation remained at a status quo until interest was renewed by growing interest in Americana.

NEW GOLDEN AGE (1970's-Present)

The 1970's saw a renewed interest in all things related to American craftsman and especially those things that were uniquely American. With this came the now famous explosion of interest in old hand-made hunting decoys and all sorts of other Americana. Good game conservation and management had begyn to pay off with rapidly increasing wildfowl populations. With these conservation efforts, heavily supported by hunters and other outdoor sportsman, came a new appreciation for what was almost lost; a new appreciation for the sheer pleasure of the hunt, a heightened awareness, if you will, of the experience of the hunt, being outdoors, enjoying it with a friend or introducing a child to the magic. What a great pleasure and satisfaction it is to introduce a non-outdoorsman friend or a child to this world, knowing that you helped bring it back and you and they will continue to practice good game management to assure it won't be lost. With all of that came the renaissance of the fine duck call. It can only get better.

A

Accomac 16
Ackerly, Lemuel and William 66
Airhart, Allen J. 223
Alfonso, Victor 123
Alford, Oscar 126
Allen, Fred A. 192, 194-195, 224
Alsop, Chip 65, 71
Anderson, W. Crew 182, 190
Anger, Ken 131, 136
Animal Trap Company 170
Ansardi, Adam 123
Arkansas Style calls 185, 192, 218-233
auctions 33

B

Backman, Edwin 47
ballast 7
banjo tail 7, 98-99
Barber Decoys 18-20
Barber, Joel 6, 8, 18-20
Barnard, Charles 81
Barnegat Bay 13, 43, 67-72
Barnes, P.K. 82
Barnes, Sam 79
Barron 17, 160
Baruch, Bernard 118, 122
battery 8
battery gun 8, 10
Bay, Frank and Jack 145
Beck, Frank 24-25
Beckhart, J.T. 185, 204, 206-207, 210,
213, 215-216
Benjon 214
Bergman, Charles 145
Bibber, Oscar 49
Birdsall, Charles 67, 172
Birdsall, Jesse 67-68
Bliss, Roswell 56, 58-59
Boice, Harry 77
books for collectors 35-39
bottom board 8, 56
Bourg, Xavier 123-124

C

Bourne, Richard A., Company 33
Bowles, A.M. 218-219
Boyd, George 49
Boyd, W.E. "Buck" 217
brands 8, 16-22, 28, 31
Bridgeport Gun and Implement Co. 200
Burgess, Ned 112-114, 116
Burke, William 211
Bush, Walter 67, 70
Butler, Sidney 48

C

Cains, Ball (Bob?) 118, 122
Cains, Hucks 118-119
Cains, Saynay 118
Cajun Call Company 223
Cajun Style calls 192, 223-225
Caldwell, Russell 182
Cameron, Glen J. 126
care of decoys 30-31
Comardelle, Alcide 124
Chadwick, Henry Keyes 46, 52, 54
Chaido, Anton and Thomas 126
Chambers, Thomas B. 21, 137-139
Chateau, Fred 17
checking 8, 30
Cobb, Elkenah 21, 106, 108
Cobb family 21, 106-111
Cobb, Nathan 21, 107-109
Cobb Island 106-111
Cochran, Ezra 217
Cochran, John 204, 207-208
comb feather painting 8
commercial carvers 1
confidence decoy 8
Connecticut 56-59
Connecticut weight 56
contemporary decoys 4, 20-24
Cook, Harry H. 145
Coombs, Frank 60, 62
Couret, Jack and Robert 123
Crandall, Horace 145

crazing 8
Crisfield 91-96
Crowell, Elmer 22, 26, 46, 51-52, 55
Currituck Island 22, 116

D

D-2 Duck Call 203-204
Dawson, John 73-74
Dawson, Walter 126
dealers 32
decorative decoys 23-26
decoy care 30-31
Delaware River School 10, 13, 44, 73-77
Delph, John 32
Denny, Sam 60-61, 63
Ditto, Charles .200
Dixie Calls 220
Dize, Elwood .91
Dodge, J.N. 17, 149-150
double shadow decoy 10
Doren, Leonard 126
Doyle Galleries, William 33
Dudley, Lee and Lem 22, 26, 112, 115
Duck Calls 180
Duet, William 123

E

Elliston, Robert 126-127
English, Dan 73-74
English, John .67
Evans Duck Decoy Company 151-153
Evans, Walter 151

F

Factory decoys 26, 46, 148-178
fakes 26-27, 29
Faulk, Clarence and Dudley 223-224
Finkel, William 137
Fisher, Elam 192-194, 200, 208
Folsom Arms Company, H.D. 226
forgeries 26-27
Frederick, George 123, 125

Fulcher, Mitchell 22, 112
Fuller, David S. (Fuller Device) 198

G

Gartner, Jake .222
Gelston, Thomas 64
Gibson, Paul .85
Glodo, Victor 192, 194, 197-199, 204, 206
Gooseville Gun Club 17
Graham, John B. 79, 82
Graves, Bert .127
Grubbs, Charles W. 192-194, 196-198
gunning scow .8

H

Haertel, Harold 126
Hancock, Clyde 218
Hancock, Miles 96-97, 101-102
Hansen, N.C. 200
Harlan, Howard 182, 190
Harlow, William F. 209-210
Harmon, Ted .32
Havre de Grace 78
Hawthorne, Dave B. 24
Hawthorne House 32
Haywood, Manny 117
Hendrickson, J. Eugene 72
Herters Inc. .154
Hiltz, Orran .47
Hobcaw Barony 114
Holmes, Benjamine 56, 58
Holly, John "Daddy" 79, 85
Hooker, Perry 213-214
Horner, Nathan Rowley 67, 71
Hudson, Ira 7, 28, 96-100
Huey, George .49

I

Illinois River School 12, 126-131
Illinois Style calls . . .193, 194-196, 200-203, 219
Indian decoys 3, 190
insurance 30
Isadore, Gaston 123

J

Jackson, Scott 83
Jantzen, "Fresh Air" Dick 145-147
Jester, Doug 97, 105
Joefrau, Charles 123, 125
Johnson, Iver 51
Johnson, Lloyd 70
Johnson, Taylor 67
Joiner, Charlie "Speed" 84
Jolly, John Edward 210-211

K

Kellum, Frank 64
Kelso, R. 213
Kenward, Henry 212
Kessler, George 126
Ketchum, Al 64
Kinney, C.L.V. 208-209
Kinney, G.D. 204
Knotts Island 114-115
Kuhlemeier, August L. 203

L

LaFrance, Mitchel 123, 125
Laing, Albert 22, 56
Lancaster, W.T. 218
Levy, Lindsey 47
Lewis, Frank 60-61
Lincoln, Joe 51-53, 112
Liu, Allan J. 31
Lockhard, Henry 86
Long Island 17, 42, 64-66
Louisiana 123-125
Louisiana Style duck calls 192, 223-225
Lovelock Cave excavations 3, 190

M

Mackey, William F. Jr. 6, 46, 131, 137
Maine 42, 49-50
Major, Chick 218, 220-221
maker brands (decoys) 8, 16-22, 28
Maryland Eastern Shore 89-90
Mason's Decoy Factory 17, 26, 145, 156-164

Massachusetts 41, 51-55, 112
McDonald, Zeke 137
McGaffey, Robert C. 137
McGrath, Brian 182, 190
McIntyre, Dick 32
McLaughlin, John 73
Melancon, J.L. 198
Meldren, Tobin 137, 139
Michigan 131-136
Mitchell, R. Madison 79, 83, 86-87
Moak, Gus 142
Mott, J. Fred Sr. 127
Mount Clemons 137, 140
Murphy, Charles F. 32

N

New Beckhart Call, The 212
New Jersey 61-66
New York State 60-63
Nichols, Davey 137
North Carolina 22, 45, 112-117
North Carolina, The 8, 71
Nova Scotia 47-48, 50

O

Ogdensburg Humpbacks 60
Old Saybrook 172
Olive, Richard W. Company 33
Olt, P.S. 203-204, 218, 221, 226
Ortley, Dipper 72

P

Pacific Coast 145-147
paddle tail 10
Padco 170
Parker, Ellis 67-68
patent model (duck calls) 184
Perdew, Charles 127, 201-203
Perkins, M.L. 13, 75
Pertuit, Dewey 123
Peterson, George 17, 149, 156
Phillips, Ed 89-90

Pickle, Leonard 215
Pickle, O.K. "Pop" 215-216
Pratt, William E.
   Manufacturing Co. 165-166, 170
punt gun 8, 10

Q

Quinn, William 75
Quogue, Long Island 64

R

raised wing carving 10, 13
Reckless, The 8, 17
Red Duck 193, 200
Reelfoot Lake Style 185, 191-192, 194,
                   204, 206, 209-217
Reeves, Phineas .137
repairs (decoys) 11, 27-29
reproductions (decoys) 23
restoration (decoys) 11, 27-29
Reynolds Double Duck Call 200
Richardson, Bob 32
Ross, Willie 49
Roussell, Remie Ange 123
Rowen, Port 137
Ruggles, Charles .126

S

Sawler, Stan 47
Schmidt, Ben 131, 134-135
Schoenhieder 127, 200
Schroeder, Tom .141
scratch feather painting 11
scull boat 11
Sears Roebuck 227
Sellers, Robert S. .87
Sellers, Walter D. .88
Shaw William T. 12, 130
shelf carving 11-12
Shourds, Harry V. 16, 67, 69
Showell, Dan 77
Sieger, Joseph 142
sink box 8, 13-14

slat body 13
Sleeper 13
Smith, Benjamine .52
sneak box 13
Sorenson, Hal 28
South Carolina 46, 118-122
Staniford, Robert H. "Rab" 172
Starr, George Ross Jr. 6, 31
St. Clair Flats 20, 131-134, 137-141
Sterling family .91-92
Sterling, Noah 91, 93-94
Stevens, H.A. Company 167-169
Stiles, Forest J. 126
Stone, Claude C. .215
Stratford (Connecticut) School 44
Strey, Frank 142, 144
Strubling, Walter 131-133
Susquehanna Flats School 78-88
Susquehanna, The 8, 17
Suydam, W.L. .17, 66

T

terminology for decoy collectors 7-14
thumb print carving 17, 96
Tongue Pincher Style calls 193, 200, 208
Toronto School 137
Turpin, Tom 198, 204-206
Tyler, Lloyd 91

U-V

user brands 16-17
values 1, 15, 27-29, 184
Verity, Obediah 64
Victor Animal Trap Company 148, 170-171
Vidacovich, Nicole 123
Virginia Eastern Shore 7, 11, 17, 96-105
Vizier, Cadis 123
Von Lengerke and Antoine (VL&A) . . .203, 226

W

Walker, Charles B. 126-127
Wallace, Amos 49
Ward Charles T. 32

Ward, David 137
Ward, Lem and Steve 26, 91, 93-95
Ward, L. Travis Sr. 93-94
Warin, George 137
Watson, Dave "Umbrella" 17, 96-97, 100
Weedman, Mark 224
Wells, John 137
West Coast 145-147
Wheeler, Charles E. "Shang" 23, 56-57
Wheeler Chauncey 60
Whipple, Mark 123, 125
Whitney, James 49
Whittaker, Nelson Price 17, 115
Wilcoxen, Perry 128
Wildfowlers Decoys, Inc. 172-178
Williams, John 112
Willingham, Jo 217-218
Wilson Augustus Aaron 49-50
wing carving 14
wing decoy or wing duck 14
Wisconsin 142-144
Wright, Alvira 112-113

X-Y-Z

Young, Dan S. 32